Graph Databases

Ian Robinson, Jim Webber, and Emil Eifrem

O'REILLY®

Beijing · Cambridge · Farnham · Köln · Sebastopol · Tokyo

Graph Databases

by Ian Robinson, Jim Webber, and Emil Eifrem

Copyright © 2013 Neo Technology, Inc.. All rights reserved.

Printed in the United States of America.

Published by O'Reilly Media, Inc., 1005 Gravenstein Highway North, Sebastopol, CA 95472.

O'Reilly books may be purchased for educational, business, or sales promotional use. Online editions are also available for most titles (*http://my.safaribooksonline.com*). For more information, contact our corporate/institutional sales department: 800-998-9938 or *corporate@oreilly.com*.

Editors: Mike Loukides and Nathan Jepson	**Indexer:** Stephen Ingle, WordCo Indexing
Production Editor: Kara Ebrahim	**Cover Designer:** Randy Comer
Copyeditor: Kim Cofer	**Interior Designer:** David Futato
Proofreader: Kevin Broccoli	**Illustrator:** Kara Ebrahim

June 2013:   First Edition

Revision History for the First Edition:

2013-05-20:   First release

See *http://oreilly.com/catalog/errata.csp?isbn=9781449356262* for release details.

ISBN: 978-1-449-35626-2

[LSI]

Table of Contents

Foreword

Graphs Are Everywhere, or the Birth of Graph Databases as We Know Them

It was 1999 and everyone worked 23-hour days. At least it felt that way. It seemed like each day brought another story about a crazy idea that just got millions of dollars in funding. All our competitors had hundreds of engineers, and we were a 20-ish person development team. As if that was not enough, 10 of our engineers spent the majority of their time just fighting the relational database.

It took us a while to figure out why. As we drilled deeper into the persistence layer of our enterprise content management application, we realized that our software was managing not just a lot of individual, isolated, and *discrete* data items, but also the *connections* between them. And while we could easily fit the discrete data in relational tables, the connected data was more challenging to store and tremendously slow to query.

Out of pure desperation, my two Neo cofounders, Johan and Peter, and I started experimenting with other models for working with data, particularly those that were centered around graphs. We were blown away by the idea that it might be possible to replace the tabular SQL semantic with a graph-centric model that would be much easier for developers to work with when navigating connected data. We sensed that, armed with a graph data model, our development team might not waste half its time fighting the database.

Surely, we said to ourselves, we can't be unique here. Graph theory has been around for nearly 300 years and is well known for its wide applicability across a number of diverse mathematical problems. Surely, there must be databases out there that embrace graphs!

Well, we Altavistad[1] around the young Web and couldn't find any. After a few months of surveying, we (naively) set out to build, from scratch, a database that worked natively with graphs. Our vision was to keep all the proven features from the relational database (transactions, ACID, triggers, etc.) but use a data model for the 21st century. Project Neo was born, and with it graph databases as we know them today.

The first decade of the new millennium has seen several world-changing new businesses spring to life, including Google, Facebook, and Twitter. And there is a common thread among them: they put connected data—graphs—at the center of their business. It's 15 years later and graphs are everywhere.

Facebook, for example, was founded on the idea that while there's value in discrete information about people—their names, what they do, etc.—there's even more value in the *relationships* between them. Facebook founder Mark Zuckerberg built an empire on the insight to capture these relationships in the *social graph*.

Similarly, Google's Larry Page and Sergey Brin figured out how to store and process not just discrete web documents, but how those web documents are connected. Google captured the *web graph*, and it made them arguably the most impactful company of the previous decade.

Today, graphs have been successfully adopted outside the web giants. One of the biggest logistics companies in the world uses a graph database in real time to route physical parcels; a major airline is leveraging graphs for its media content metadata; and a top-tier financial services firm has rewritten its entire entitlements infrastructure on Neo4j. Virtually unknown a few years ago, graph databases are now used in industries as diverse as healthcare, retail, oil and gas, media, gaming, and beyond, with every indication of accelerating their already explosive pace.

These ideas deserve a new breed of tools: general-purpose database management technologies that embrace connected data and enable graph thinking, which are the kind of tools I wish had been available off the shelf when we were fighting the relational database back in 1999.

I hope this book will serve as a great introduction to this wonderful emerging world of graph technologies, and I hope it will inspire you to start using a graph database in your next project so that you too can unlock the extraordinary power of graphs. Good luck!

—Emil Eifrem
Cofounder of Neo4j and CEO of Neo Technology
Menlo Park, California
May 2013

---

1. For the younger readers, it may come as a shock that there was a time in the history of mankind when Google didn't exist. Back then, dinosaurs ruled the earth and search engines with names like Altavista, Lycos, and Excite were used, primarily to find ecommerce portals for pet food on the Internet.

Preface

Graph databases address one of the great macroscopic business trends of today: leveraging complex and dynamic relationships in highly connected data to generate insight and competitive advantage. Whether we want to understand relationships between customers, elements in a telephone or data center network, entertainment producers and consumers, or genes and proteins, the ability to understand and analyze vast graphs of highly connected data will be key in determining which companies outperform their competitors over the coming decade.

For data of any significant size or value, graph databases are the best way to represent and query connected data. Connected data is data whose interpretation and value requires us first to understand the ways in which its constituent elements are related. More often than not, to generate this understanding, we need to name and qualify the connections between things.

Although large corporates realized this some time ago and began creating their own proprietary graph processing technologies, we're now in an era where that technology has rapidly become democratized. Today, general-purpose graph databases are a reality, enabling mainstream users to experience the benefits of connected data without having to invest in building their own graph infrastructure.

What's remarkable about this renaissance of graph data and graph thinking is that graph theory itself is not new. Graph theory was pioneered by Euler in the 18th century, and has been actively researched and improved by mathematicians, sociologists, anthropologists, and others ever since. However, it is only in the past few years that graph theory and graph thinking have been applied to information management. In that time, graph databases have helped solve important problems in the areas of social networking, master data management, geospatial, recommendations, and more. This increased focus on graph databases is driven by twin forces: by the massive commercial success of companies such as Facebook, Google, and Twitter, all of whom have centered their business models around their own proprietary graph technologies; and by the introduction of general-purpose graph databases into the technology landscape.

About This Book

The purpose of this book is to introduce graphs and graph databases to technology practitioners, including developers, database professionals, and technology decision makers. Reading this book will give you a practical understanding of graph databases. We show how the graph model "shapes" data, and how we query, reason about, understand, and *act upon* data using a graph database. We discuss the kinds of problems that are well aligned with graph databases, with examples drawn from actual real-world use cases, and we show how to plan and implement a graph database solution.

Conventions Used in This Book

The following typographical conventions are used in this book:

Italic
:   Indicates new terms, URLs, email addresses, filenames, and file extensions.

`Constant width`
:   Used for program listings, as well as within paragraphs to refer to program elements such as variable or function names, databases, data types, environment variables, statements, and keywords.

`Constant width bold`
:   Shows commands or other text that should be typed literally by the user.

`Constant width italic`
:   Shows text that should be replaced with user-supplied values or by values determined by context.

This icon signifies a tip, suggestion, or general note.

This icon indicates a warning or caution.

Using Code Examples

This book is here to help you get your job done. In general, if this book includes code examples, you may use the code in this book in your programs and documentation. You do not need to contact us for permission unless you're reproducing a significant portion of the code. For example, writing a program that uses several chunks of code from this book does not require permission. Selling or distributing a CD-ROM of examples from

O'Reilly books does require permission. Answering a question by citing this book and quoting example code does not require permission. Incorporating a significant amount of example code from this book into your product's documentation does require permission.

We appreciate, but do not require, attribution. An attribution usually includes the title, author, publisher, and ISBN. For example: "*Graph Databases* by Ian Robinson, Jim Webber, and Emil Eifrem (O'Reilly). Copyright 2013 Neo Technology, Inc., 978-1-449-35626-2."

If you feel your use of code examples falls outside fair use or the permission given above, feel free to contact us at *permissions@oreilly.com*.

Safari® Books Online

 Safari Books Online is an on-demand digital library that delivers expert content in both book and video form from the world's leading authors in technology and business.

Technology professionals, software developers, web designers, and business and creative professionals use Safari Books Online as their primary resource for research, problem solving, learning, and certification training.

Safari Books Online offers a range of product mixes and pricing programs for organizations, government agencies, and individuals. Subscribers have access to thousands of books, training videos, and prepublication manuscripts in one fully searchable database from publishers like O'Reilly Media, Prentice Hall Professional, Addison-Wesley Professional, Microsoft Press, Sams, Que, Peachpit Press, Focal Press, Cisco Press, John Wiley & Sons, Syngress, Morgan Kaufmann, IBM Redbooks, Packt, Adobe Press, FT Press, Apress, Manning, New Riders, McGraw-Hill, Jones & Bartlett, Course Technology, and dozens more. For more information about Safari Books Online, please visit us online.

How to Contact Us

Please address comments and questions concerning this book to the publisher:

O'Reilly Media, Inc.
1005 Gravenstein Highway North
Sebastopol, CA 95472
800-998-9938 (in the United States or Canada)
707-829-0515 (international or local)
707-829-0104 (fax)

We have a web page for this book, where we list errata, examples, and any additional information. You can access this page at *http://oreil.ly/graph-databases*.

To comment or ask technical questions about this book, send email to *bookques tions@oreilly.com*.

For more information about our books, courses, conferences, and news, see our website at *http://www.oreilly.com*.

Find us on Facebook: *http://facebook.com/oreilly*

Follow us on Twitter: *http://twitter.com/oreillymedia*

Watch us on YouTube: *http://www.youtube.com/oreillymedia*

Acknowledgments

We would like to thank our technical reviewers: Michael Hunger, Colin Jack, Mark Needham, and Pramod Sadalage.

Our appreciation and thanks to our editor, Nathan Jepson.

Our colleagues at Neo Technology have contributed enormously of their time, experience, and effort throughout the writing of this book. Thanks in particular go to Anders Nawroth, for his invaluable assistance with our book's toolchain; Andrés Taylor, for his enthusiastic help with all things Cypher; and Philip Rathle, for his advice and contributions to the text.

A big thank you to everyone in the Neo4j community for your many contributions to the graph database space over the years.

And special thanks to our families, for their love and support: Lottie, Tiger, Elliot, Kath, Billy, Madelene, and Noomi.

CHAPTER 1

Introduction

Although much of this book talks about graph data models, it is not a book about graph theory.[1] We don't need much theory to take advantage of graph databases: provided we understand what a graph is, we're practically there. With that in mind, let's refresh our memories about graphs in general.

What Is a Graph?

Formally, a graph is just a collection of *vertices* and *edges*—or, in less intimidating language, a set of *nodes* and the *relationships* that connect them. Graphs represent entities as nodes and the ways in which those entities relate to the world as relationships. This general-purpose, expressive structure allows us to model all kinds of scenarios, from the construction of a space rocket, to a system of roads, and from the supply-chain or provenance of foodstuff, to medical history for populations, and beyond.

Graphs Are Everywhere

Graphs are extremely useful in understanding a wide diversity of datasets in fields such as science, government, and business. The real world—unlike the forms-based model behind the relational database—is rich and interrelated: uniform and rule-bound in parts, exceptional and irregular in others. Once we understand graphs, we begin to see them in all sorts of places. Gartner (*http://www.gartner.com/id=2081316*), for example, identifies five graphs in the world of business—social, intent, consumption, interest, and

---

1. For introductions to graph theory, see Richard J. Trudeau, *Introduction To Graph Theory* (Dover, 1993) and Gary Chartrand, *Introductory Graph Theory* (Dover, 1985). For an excellent introduction to how graphs provide insight into complex events and behaviors, see David Easley and Jon Kleinberg, *Networks, Crowds, and Markets: Reasoning about a Highly Connected World* (Cambridge University Press, 2010).

mobile—and says that the ability to leverage these graphs provides a "sustainable competitive advantage."

For example, Twitter's data is easily represented as a graph. In Figure 1-1 we see a small network of followers. The relationships are key here in establishing the semantic context: namely, that Billy follows Harry, and that Harry, in turn, follows Billy. Ruth and Harry likewise follow each other, but sadly, although Ruth follows Billy, Billy hasn't (yet) reciprocated.

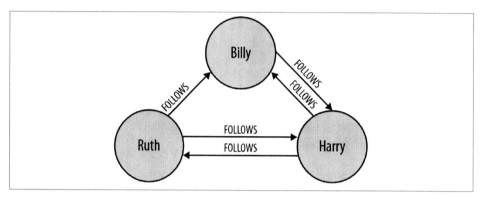

Figure 1-1. A small social graph

Of course, Twitter's real graph is hundreds of millions of times larger than the example in Figure 1-1, but it works on precisely the same principles. In Figure 1-2 we've expanded the graph to include the messages published by Ruth.

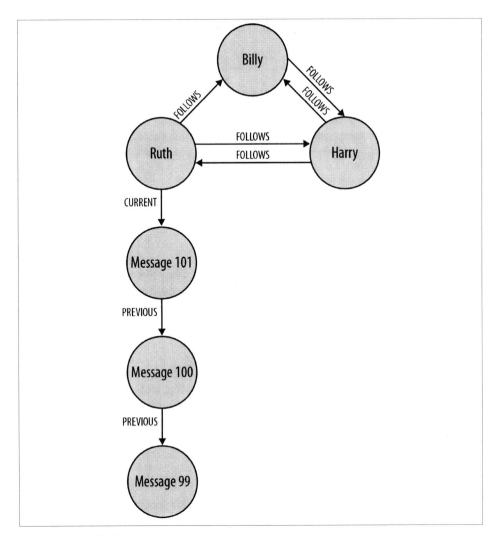

Figure 1-2. Publishing messages

Though simple, Figure 1-2 shows the expressive power of the graph model. It's easy to see that Ruth has published a string of messages. The most recent message can be found by following a relationship marked CURRENT; PREVIOUS relationships then create a time line of posts.

The Property Graph Model

In discussing Figure 1-2 we've also informally introduced the most popular variant of graph model, the *property graph* (in Appendix A, we discuss alternative graph data models in more detail). A property graph has the following characteristics:

- It contains nodes and relationships
- Nodes contain properties (key-value pairs)
- Relationships are named and directed, and always have a start and end node
- Relationships can also contain properties

Most people find the property graph model intuitive and easy to understand. Although simple, it can be used to describe the overwhelming majority of graph use cases in ways that yield useful insights into our data.

A High-Level View of the Graph Space

Numerous projects and products for managing, processing, and analyzing graphs have exploded onto the scene in recent years. The sheer number of technologies makes it difficult to keep track of these tools and how they differ, even for those of us who are active in the space. This section provides a high-level framework for making sense of the emerging graph landscape.

From 10,000 feet we can divide the graph space into two parts:

Technologies used primarily for transactional online graph persistence, typically accessed directly in real time from an application
> These technologies are called *graph databases* and are the main focus of this book. They are the equivalent of "normal" online transactional processing (OLTP) databases in the relational world.

Technologies used primarily for offline graph analytics, typically performed as a series of batch steps
> These technologies can be called *graph compute engines*. They can be thought of as being in the same category as other technologies for analysis of data in bulk, such as data mining and online analytical processing (OLAP).

Another way to slice the graph space is to look at the graph models employed by the various technologies. There are three dominant graph data models: the property graph, Resource Description Framework (RDF) triples, and hypergraphs. We describe these in detail in Appendix A. Most of the popular graph databases on the market use the property graph model, and in consequence, it's the model we'll use throughout the remainder of this book.

Graph Databases

A *graph database* management system (henceforth, a graph database) is an online database management system with Create, Read, Update, and Delete (CRUD) methods that expose a graph data model. Graph databases are generally built for use with transactional (OLTP) systems. Accordingly, they are normally optimized for transactional performance, and engineered with transactional integrity and operational availability in mind.

There are two properties of graph databases you should consider when investigating graph database technologies:

The underlying storage

Some graph databases use *native graph storage* that is optimized and designed for storing and managing graphs. Not all graph database technologies use native graph storage, however. Some serialize the graph data into a relational database, an object-oriented database, or some other general-purpose data store.

The processing engine

Some definitions require that a graph database use *index-free adjacency*, meaning that connected nodes physically "point" to each other in the database.[2] Here we take a slightly broader view: any database that from the user's perspective *behaves* like a graph database (i.e., exposes a graph data model through CRUD operations) qualifies as a graph database. We do acknowledge, however, the significant performance advantages of index-free adjacency, and therefore use the term *native graph processing* to describe graph databases that leverage index-free adjacency.

---

2. See Rodriguez, M.A., Neubauer, P., "The Graph Traversal Pattern," 2010 (*http://arxiv.org/abs/1004.1001*).

It's important to note that native graph storage and native graph processing are neither good nor bad—they're simply classic engineering trade-offs. The benefit of native graph storage is that its purpose-built stack is engineered for performance and scalability. The benefit of non-native graph storage, in contrast, is that it typically depends on a mature nongraph backend (such as MySQL) whose production characteristics are well understood by operations teams. Native graph processing (index-free adjacency) benefits traversal performance, but at the expense of making some nontraversal queries difficult or memory intensive.

Relationships are first-class citizens of the graph data model, unlike other database management systems, which require us to infer connections between entities using contrived properties such as foreign keys, or out-of-band processing like map-reduce. By assembling the simple abstractions of nodes and relationships into connected structures, graph databases enable us to build arbitrarily sophisticated models that map closely to our problem domain. The resulting models are simpler and at the same time more expressive than those produced using traditional relational databases and the other NOSQL stores.

Figure 1-3 shows a pictorial overview of some of the graph databases on the market today based on their storage and processing models.

Graph Compute Engines

A *graph compute engine* is a technology that enables global graph computational algorithms to be run against large datasets. Graph compute engines are designed to do things like identify clusters in your data, or answer questions such as, "how many relationships, on average, does everyone in a social network have?"

Because of their emphasis on global queries, graph compute engines are normally optimized for scanning and processing large amounts of information in batch, and in that respect they are similar to other batch analysis technologies, such as data mining and OLAP, that are familiar in the relational world. Whereas some graph compute engines include a graph storage layer, others (and arguably most) concern themselves strictly with processing data that is fed in from an external source, and returning the results.

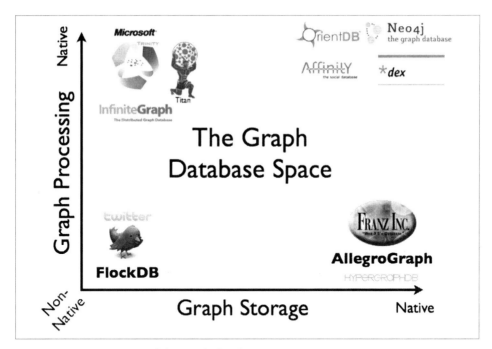

Figure 1-3. An overview of the graph database space

Figure 1-4 shows a common architecture for deploying a graph compute engine. The architecture includes a system of record (SOR) database with OLTP properties (such as MySQL, Oracle, or Neo4j), which serves, requests, and responds to queries from the application (and ultimately the users) at runtime. Periodically, an Extract, Transform, and Load (ETL) job moves data from the system of record database into the graph compute engine for offline querying and analysis.

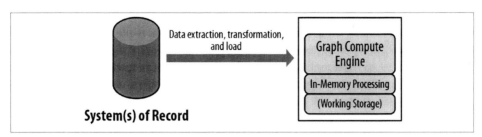

Figure 1-4. A high-level view of a typical graph compute engine deployment

A variety of different types of graph compute engines exist. Most notably there are *in-memory/single machine* graph compute engines like Cassovary (*https://github.com/twitter/cassovary*), and *distributed* graph compute engines like Pegasus (*http://www.cs.cmu.edu/~pegasus/*) or Giraph (*http://incubator.apache.org/giraph/*). Most distributed graph compute engines are based on the Pregel (*http://dl.acm.org/cita tion.cfm?id=1807184*) white paper, authored by Google, which describes the graph compute engine Google uses to rank pages.

This Book Focuses on Graph Databases

The previous section provided a course-grained overview of the entire graph space. The rest of this book focuses on graph databases. Our goal throughout is to describe graph database *concepts*. Where appropriate, we illustrate these concepts with examples drawn from our experience of developing solutions using the property graph model and the Neo4j database. Irrespective of the graph model or database used for the examples, however, the important concepts carry over to other graph databases.

The Power of Graph Databases

Notwithstanding the fact that just about anything can be modeled as a graph, we live in a pragmatic world of budgets, project time lines, corporate standards, and commoditized skillsets. That a graph database provides a powerful but novel data modeling technique does not in itself provide sufficient justification for replacing a well-established, well-understood data platform; there must also be an immediate and very significant practical benefit. In the case of graph databases, this motivation exists in the form of a set of use cases and data patterns whose performance improves by one or more orders of magnitude when implemented in a graph, and whose latency is much lower compared to batch processing of aggregates. On top of this performance benefit, graph databases offer an extremely flexible data model, and a mode of delivery aligned with today's agile software delivery practices.

Performance

One compelling reason, then, for choosing a graph database is the sheer performance increase when dealing with connected data versus relational databases and NOSQL stores. In contrast to relational databases, where join-intensive query performance deteriorates as the dataset gets bigger, with a graph database performance tends to remain relatively constant, even as the dataset grows. This is because queries are localized to a portion of the graph. As a result, the execution time for each query is proportional only to the size of the part of the graph traversed to satisfy that query, rather than the size of the overall graph.

Flexibility

As developers and data architects we want to connect data as the domain dictates, thereby allowing structure and schema to emerge in tandem with our growing understanding of the problem space, rather than being imposed upfront, when we know least about the real shape and intricacies of the data. Graph databases address this want directly. As we show in Chapter 3, the graph data model expresses and accommodates business needs in a way that enables IT to *move at the speed of business*.

Graphs are naturally additive, meaning we can add new kinds of relationships, new nodes, and new subgraphs to an existing structure without disturbing existing queries and application functionality. These things have generally positive implications for developer productivity and project risk. Because of the graph model's flexibility, we don't have to model our domain in exhaustive detail ahead of time—a practice that is all but foolhardy in the face of changing business requirements. The additive nature of graphs also means we tend to perform fewer migrations, thereby reducing maintenance overhead and risk.

Agility

We want to be able to evolve our data model in step with the rest of our application, using a technology aligned with today's incremental and iterative software delivery practices. Modern graph databases equip us to perform frictionless development and graceful systems maintenance. In particular, the schema-free nature of the graph data model, coupled with the testable nature of a graph database's application programming interface (API) and query language, empower us to evolve an application in a controlled manner.

At the same time, precisely because they are schema free, graph databases lack the kind of schema-oriented data governance mechanisms we're familiar with in the relational world. But this is not a risk; rather, it calls forth a far more visible and actionable kind of governance. As we show in Chapter 4, governance is typically applied in a programmatic fashion, using tests to drive out the data model and queries, as well as assert the business rules that depend upon the graph. This is no longer a controversial practice: more so than relational development, graph database development aligns well with today's agile and test-driven software development practices, allowing graph database–backed applications to evolve in step with changing business environments.

Summary

In this chapter we've reviewed the graph property model, a simple yet expressive tool for representing connected data. Property graphs capture complex domains in an expressive and flexible fashion, while graph databases make it easy to develop applications that manipulate our graph models.

In the next chapter we'll look in more detail at how several different technologies address the challenge of connected data, starting with relational databases, moving onto aggregate NOSQL stores, and ending with graph databases. In the course of the discussion, we'll see why graphs and graph databases provide the best means for modeling, storing, and querying connected data. Later chapters then go on to show how to design and implement a graph database–based solution.

CHAPTER 2

Options for Storing Connected Data

We live in a connected world. To thrive and progress, we need to understand and influence the web of connections that surrounds us.

How do today's technologies deal with the challenge of connected data? In this chapter we look at how relational databases and aggregate NOSQL stores manage graphs and connected data, and compare their performance to that of a graph database. For readers interested in exploring the topic of NOSQL, Appendix A describes the four major types of NOSQL databases.

Relational Databases Lack Relationships

For several decades, developers have tried to accommodate connected, semi-structured datasets inside relational databases. But whereas relational databases were initially designed to codify paper forms and tabular structures—something they do exceedingly well—they struggle when attempting to model the ad hoc, exceptional relationships that crop up in the real world. Ironically, relational databases deal poorly with relationships.

Relationships do exist in the vernacular of relational databases, but only as a means of joining tables. In our discussion of connected data in the previous chapter, we mentioned we often need to disambiguate the semantics of the relationships that connect entities, as well as qualify their weight or strength. Relational relations do nothing of the sort. Worse still, as outlier data multiplies, and the overall structure of the dataset becomes more complex and less uniform, the relational model becomes burdened with large join tables, sparsely populated rows, and lots of null-checking logic. The rise in connectedness translates in the relational world into increased joins, which impede performance and make it difficult for us to evolve an existing database in response to changing business needs.

Figure 2-1 shows a relational schema for storing customer orders in a customer-centric, transactional application.

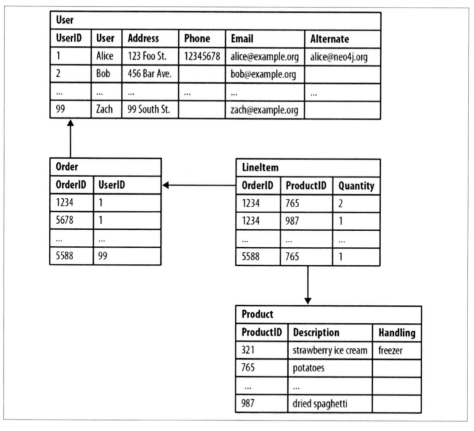

User					
UserID	User	Address	Phone	Email	Alternate
1	Alice	123 Foo St.	12345678	alice@example.org	alice@neo4j.org
2	Bob	456 Bar Ave.		bob@example.org	
...	...	...	...	...	...
99	Zach	99 South St.		zach@example.org	

Order	
OrderID	UserID
1234	1
5678	1
...	...
5588	99

LineItem		
OrderID	ProductID	Quantity
1234	765	2
1234	987	1
...	...	...
5588	765	1

Product		
ProductID	Description	Handling
321	strawberry ice cream	freezer
765	potatoes	
...	...	
987	dried spaghetti	

Figure 2-1. Semantic relationships are hidden in a relational database

The application exerts a tremendous influence over the design of this schema, making some queries very easy, and others more difficult:

- Join tables add accidental complexity; they mix business data with foreign key metadata.

- Foreign key constraints add additional development and maintenance overhead *just to make the database work.*

- Sparse tables with nullable columns require special checking in code, despite the presence of a schema.

- Several *expensive* joins are needed just to discover what a customer bought.

- Reciprocal queries are even more costly. "What products did a customer buy?" is relatively cheap compared to "which customers bought this product?", which is the basis of recommendation systems. We could introduce an index, but even with an index, recursive questions such as "which customers bought this product who also bought that product?" quickly become prohibitively expensive as the degree of recursion increases.

Relational databases struggle with highly connected domains. To understand the cost of performing connected queries in a relational database, we'll look at some simple and not-so-simple queries in a social network domain.

Figure 2-2 shows a simple join-table arrangement for recording friendships.

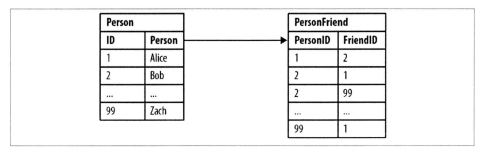

Figure 2-2. Modeling friends and friends-of-friends in a relational database

Asking "who are Bob's friends?" is easy, as shown in Example 2-1.

Example 2-1. Bob's friends

```
SELECT p1.Person
FROM Person p1 JOIN PersonFriend
  ON PersonFriend.FriendID = p1.ID
JOIN Person p2
  ON PersonFriend.PersonID = p2.ID
WHERE p2.Person = 'Bob'
```

Based on our sample data, the answer is Alice and Zach. This isn't a particularly expensive or difficult query, because it constrains the number of rows under consideration using the filter WHERE Person.person='Bob'.

Friendship isn't always a reflexive relationship, so in Example 2-2, we ask the reciprocal query, which is, "who is friends with Bob?"

Example 2-2. Who is friends with Bob?

```
SELECT p1.Person
FROM Person p1 JOIN PersonFriend
  ON PersonFriend.PersonID = p1.ID
JOIN Person p2
  ON PersonFriend.FriendID = p2.ID
WHERE p2.Person = 'Bob'
```

The answer to this query is `Alice`; sadly, `Zach` doesn't consider `Bob` to be a friend. This reciprocal query is still easy to implement, but on the database side it's more expensive, because the database now has to consider all the rows in the `PersonFriend` table.

We can add an index, but this still involves an expensive layer of indirection. Things become even more problematic when we ask, "who are the friends of my friends?" Hierarchies in SQL use recursive joins, which make the query syntactically and computationally more complex, as shown in Example 2-3. (Some relational databases provide syntactic sugar for this—for instance, Oracle has a `CONNECT BY` function—which simplifies the query, but not the underlying computational complexity.)

Example 2-3. Alice's friends-of-friends

```
SELECT p1.Person AS PERSON, p2.Person AS FRIEND_OF_FRIEND
FROM PersonFriend pf1 JOIN Person p1
  ON pf1.PersonID = p1.ID
JOIN PersonFriend pf2
  ON pf2.PersonID = pf1.FriendID
JOIN Person p2
  ON pf2.FriendID = p2.ID
WHERE p1.Person = 'Alice' AND pf2.FriendID <> p1.ID
```

This query is computationally complex, even though it only deals with the friends of Alice's friends, and goes no deeper into Alice's social network. Things get more complex and more expensive the deeper we go into the network. Though it's possible get an answer to the question "who are my friends-of-friends-of-friends?" in a reasonable period of time, queries that extend to four, five, or six degrees of friendship deteriorate significantly due to the computational and space complexity of recursively joining tables.

We work against the grain whenever we try to model and query connectedness in a relational database. Besides the query and computational complexity just outlined, we also have to deal with the double-edged sword of schema. More often than not, schema proves to be both rigid and brittle. To subvert its rigidity we create sparsely populated tables with many nullable columns, and code to handle the exceptional cases—all because there's no real one-size-fits-all schema to accommodate the variety in the data we encounter. This increases coupling and all but destroys any semblance of cohesion. Its brittleness manifests itself as the extra effort and care required to migrate from one schema to another as an application evolves.

NOSQL Databases Also Lack Relationships

Most NOSQL databases—whether key-value-, document-, or column-oriented—store sets of disconnected documents/values/columns. This makes it difficult to use them for connected data and graphs.

One well-known strategy for adding relationships to such stores is to embed an aggregate's identifier inside the field belonging to another aggregate—effectively introducing foreign keys. But this requires joining aggregates at the application level, which quickly becomes prohibitively expensive.

When we look at an aggregate store model, such as the one in Figure 2-3, we conjure up relationships. Seeing a reference to order: 1234 in the record beginning user: Alice, we infer a connection between user: Alice and order: 1234. This gives us false hope that we can use keys and values to manage graphs.

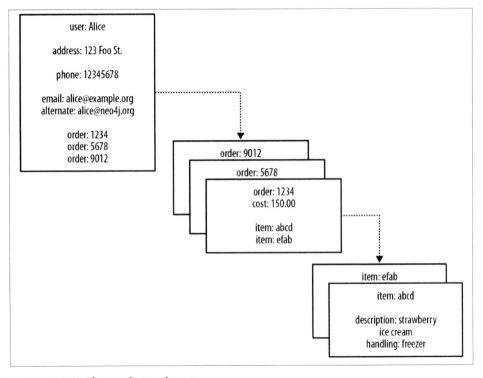

Figure 2-3. Reifying relationships in an aggregate store

In Figure 2-3 we infer that some property values are really references to foreign aggregates elsewhere in the database. But turning these inferences into a navigable structure doesn't come for free, because relationships *between* aggregates aren't first-class citizens in the data model—most aggregate stores furnish only the *insides* of aggregates with structure, in the form of nested maps. Instead, the application that uses the database must build relationships from these flat, disconnected data structures. We also have to ensure the application updates or deletes these foreign aggregate references in tandem with the rest of the data; if this doesn't happen, the store will accumulate dangling references, which can harm data quality and query performance.

Links and Walking

The Riak key-value store allows each of its stored values to be augmented with link metadata. Each link is one-way, pointing from one stored value to another. Riak allows any number of these links to be *walked* (in Riak terminology), making the model somewhat connected. However, this link walking is powered by map-reduce, which is relatively latent. Unlike a graph database, this linking is suitable only for simple graph-structured programming rather than general graph algorithms.

There's another weak point in this scheme. Because there are no identifiers that "point" backward (the foreign aggregate "links" are not reflexive, of course), we lose the ability to run other interesting queries on the database. For example, with the structure shown in Figure 2-3, asking the database who has bought a particular product—perhaps for the purpose of making a recommendation based on customer profile—is an expensive operation. If we want to answer this kind of question, we will likely end up exporting the dataset and processing it via some external compute infrastructure, such as Hadoop, to brute-force compute the result. Alternatively, we can retrospectively insert backward-pointing foreign aggregate references, before then querying for the result. Either way, the results will be latent.

It's tempting to think that aggregate stores are functionally equivalent to graph databases with respect to connected data. But this is not the case. Aggregate stores do not maintain consistency of connected data, nor do they support what is known as *index-free adjacency*, whereby elements contain direct links to their neighbors. As a result, for connected data problems, aggregate stores must employ inherently latent methods for creating and querying relationships outside the data model.

Let's see how some of these limitations manifest themselves. Figure 2-4 shows a small social network as implemented using documents in an aggregate store.

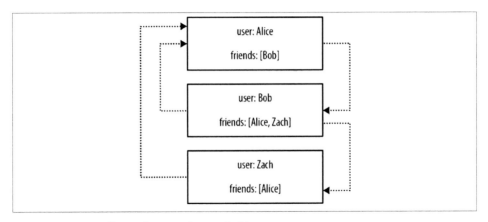

Figure 2-4. A small social network encoded in an aggregate store

With this structure, it's easy to find a user's immediate friends—assuming, of course, the application has been diligent in ensuring identifiers stored in the friends property are consistent with other record IDs in the database. In this case we simply look up immediate friends by their ID, which requires numerous index lookups (one for each friend) but no brute-force scans of the entire dataset. Doing this, we'd find, for example, that Bob considers Alice and Zach to be friends.

But friendship isn't always reflexive. What if we'd like to ask "who is friends with Bob?" rather than "who are Bob's friends?" That's a more difficult question to answer, and in this case our only option would be to brute-force scan across the whole dataset looking for friends entries that contain Bob.

O-Notation and Brute-Force Processing

We use O-notation as a shorthand way of describing how the performance of an algorithm changes with the size of the dataset. An *O(1)* algorithm exhibits constant-time performance; that is, the algorithm takes the same time to execute irrespective of the size of the dataset. An *O(n)* algorithm exhibits linear performance; when the dataset doubles, the time taken to execute the algorithm doubles. An *O(log n)* algorithm exhibits logarithmic performance; when the dataset doubles, the time taken to execute the algorithm increases by a fixed amount. The relative performance increase may appear costly when a dataset is in its infancy, but it quickly tails off as the dataset gets a lot bigger. An *O(m log n)* algorithm is the most costly of the ones considered in this book. With an *O(m log n)* algorithm, when the dataset doubles, the execution time doubles *and* increments by some additional amount proportional to the number of elements in the dataset.

Brute-force computing an entire dataset is *O(n)* in terms of complexity because all *n* aggregates in the data store must be considered. That's far too costly for most reasonable-sized datasets, where we'd prefer an *O(log n)* algorithm—which is somewhat efficient because it discards half the potential workload on each iteration—or better.

Conversely, a graph database provides constant order lookup for the same query. In this case, we simply find the node in the graph that represents Bob, and then follow any incoming *friend* relationships; these relationships lead to nodes that represent people who consider Bob to be their friend. This is far cheaper than brute-forcing the result because it considers far fewer members of the network; that is, it considers only those that are connected to Bob. Of course, if everybody is friends with Bob, we'll still end up considering the entire dataset.

To avoid having to process the entire dataset, we could denormalize the storage model by adding backward links. Adding a second property, called perhaps `friended_by`, to each user, we can list the incoming friendship relations associated with that user. But this doesn't come for free. For starters, we have to pay the initial and ongoing cost of increased write latency, plus the increased disk utilization cost for storing the additional metadata. On top of that, *traversing* the links remains expensive, because each hop requires an index lookup. This is because aggregates have no notion of locality, unlike graph databases, which naturally provide index-free adjacency through real—not reified —relationships. By implementing a graph structure atop a nonnative store, we get some of the benefits of partial connectedness, but at substantial cost.

This substantial cost is amplified when it comes to traversing deeper than just one hop. Friends are easy enough, but imagine trying to compute—in real time—friends-of-friends, or friends-of-friends-of-friends. That's impractical with this kind of database because traversing a fake relationship isn't cheap. This not only limits your chances of expanding your social network, but it reduces profitable recommendations, misses faulty equipment in your data center, and lets fraudulent purchasing activity slip through the net. Many systems try to maintain the appearance of graph-like processing, but inevitably it's done in batches and doesn't provide the real-time interaction that users demand.

Graph Databases Embrace Relationships

The previous examples have dealt with *implicitly* connected data. As users we infer semantic dependencies between entities, but the data models—and the databases themselves—are blind to these connections. To compensate, our applications must create a network out of the flat, disconnected data at hand, and then deal with any slow queries and latent writes across denormalized stores that arise.

What we really want is a cohesive picture of the whole, including the connections between elements. In contrast to the stores we've just looked at, in the graph world, connected data is *stored as connected data*. Where there are connections in the domain, there are connections in the data. For example, consider the social network shown in Figure 2-5.

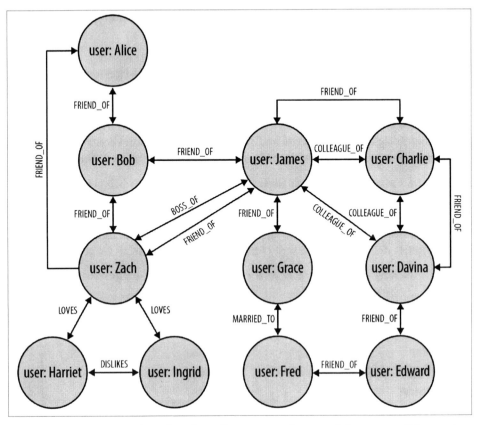

Figure 2-5. Easily modeling friends, colleagues, workers, and (unrequited) lovers in a graph

In this social network, as in so many real-world cases of connected data, the connections between entities don't exhibit uniformity across the domain—the domain is semi-structured. A social network is a popular example of a densely connected, semi-structured network, one that resists being captured by a one-size-fits-all schema or conveniently split across disconnected aggregates. Our simple network of friends has grown in size (there are now potential friends up to six degrees away) and expressive richness. The flexibility of the graph model has allowed us to add new *nodes* and new *relationships* without compromising the existing network or migrating data—the original data and its intent remain intact.

The graph offers a much richer picture of the network. We can see who LOVES whom (and whether that love is requited). We can see who is a COLLEAGUE_OF of whom, and who is BOSS_OF them all. We can see who's off the market, because they're MARRIED_TO someone else; we can even see the antisocial elements in our otherwise social network, as represented by DISLIKES relationships. With this graph at our disposal, we can now look at the performance advantages of graph databases when dealing with connected data.

Relationships in a graph naturally form paths. Querying—or traversing—the graph involves following paths. Because of the fundamentally path-oriented nature of the data model, the majority of path-based graph database operations are highly aligned with the way in which the data is laid out, making them extremely efficient. In their book *Neo4j in Action* (*http://www.manning.com/partner/*), Partner and Vukotic perform an experiment using a relational store and Neo4j. The comparison shows that the graph database is substantially quicker for connected data than a relational store.

Partner and Vukotic's experiment seeks to find friends-of-friends in a social network, to a maximum depth of five. Given any two persons chosen at random, is there a path that connects them that is at most five relationships long? For a social network containing 1,000,000 people, each with approximately 50 friends, the results strongly suggest that graph databases are the best choice for connected data, as we see in Table 2-1.

Table 2-1. Finding extended friends in a relational database versus efficient finding in Neo4j

Depth	RDBMS execution time (s)	Neo4j execution time (s)	Records returned
2	0.016	0.01	~2500
3	30.267	0.168	~110,000
4	1543.505	1.359	~600,000
5	Unfinished	2.132	~800,000

At depth two (friends-of-friends), both the relational database and the graph database perform well enough for us to consider using them in an online system. Although the Neo4j query runs in two-thirds the time of the relational one, an end user would barely notice the difference in milliseconds between the two. By the time we reach depth three (friend-of-friend-of-friend), however, it's clear that the relational database can no longer deal with the query in a reasonable time frame: the 30 seconds it takes to complete would be completely unacceptable for an online system. In contrast, Neo4j's response time remains relatively flat: just a fraction of a second to perform the query—definitely quick enough for an online system.

At depth four the relational database exhibits crippling latency, making it practically useless for an online system. Neo4j's timings have deteriorated a little too, but the latency here is at the periphery of being acceptable for a responsive online system. Finally, at depth five, the relational database simply takes too long to complete the query. Neo4j, in contrast, returns a result in around two seconds. At depth five, it turns out that almost the entire network is our friend: because of this, for many real-world use cases, we'd likely trim the results, and the timings.

 Both aggregate stores and relational databases perform poorly when we move away from modestly sized set operations—operations that they should both be good at. Things slow down when we try to mine path information from the graph, as with the friends-of-friends example. We don't mean to unduly beat up on either aggregate stores or relational databases; they have a fine technology pedigree for the things they're good at, but they fall short when managing connected data. Anything more than a shallow traversal of immediate friends, or possibly friends-of-friends, will be slow because of the number of index lookups involved. Graphs, on the other hand, use index-free adjacency to ensure that traversing connected data is extremely rapid.

The social network example helps illustrate how different technologies deal with connected data, but is it a valid use case? Do we really need to find such remote "friends"? Perhaps not. But substitute social networks for any other domain, and you'll see we experience similar performance, modeling, and maintenance benefits. Whether music or data center management, bio-informatics or football statistics, network sensors or time-series of trades, graphs provide powerful insight into our data. Let's look, then, at another contemporary application of graphs: recommending products based on a user's purchase history and the histories of his friends, neighbors, and other people like him. With this example, we'll bring together several independent facets of a user's lifestyle to make accurate and profitable recommendations.

We'll start by modeling the purchase history of a user as connected data. In a graph, this is as simple as linking the user to her orders, and linking orders together to provide a purchase history, as shown in Figure 2-6.

The graph shown in Figure 2-6 provides a great deal of insight into customer behavior. We can see all the orders a user has PLACED, and we can easily reason about what each order CONTAINS. So far so good. But on top of that, we've enriched the graph to support well-known access patterns. For example, users often want to see their order history, so we've added a linked list structure to the graph that allows us to find a user's most recent order by following an outgoing MOST_RECENT relationship. We can then iterate through the list, going further back in time, by following each PREVIOUS relationship. If we want to move forward in time, we can follow each PREVIOUS relationship in the opposite direction, or add a reciprocal NEXT relationship.

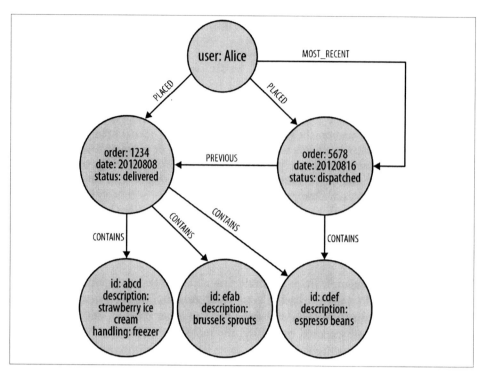

Figure 2-6. Modeling a user's order history in a graph

Now we can start to make recommendations. If we notice that users who buy strawberry ice cream also buy espresso beans, we can start to recommend those beans to users who normally only buy the ice cream. But this is a rather one-dimensional recommendation, even if we traverse lots of orders to ensure there's a strong correlation between strawberry ice cream and espresso beans. We can do *much* better. To increase our graph's power, we can join it to graphs from other domains. Because graphs are naturally multi-dimensional structures, it's then quite straightforward to ask more sophisticated questions of the data to gain access to a fine-tuned market segment. For example, we can ask the graph to find for us "all the flavors of ice cream liked by people who live near a user, and enjoy espresso, but dislike Brussels sprouts."

For the purpose of our interpretation of the data, we can consider the degree to which someone repeatedly buys a product to be indicative of whether or not he likes that product. But how might we define "living near"? Well, it turns out that geospatial co-ordinates are best modeled as graphs. One of the most popular structures for representing geospatial coordinates is called an *R-Tree*. An R-Tree (*http://en.wikipedia.org/wiki/R-tree*) is a graph-like index that describes bounded boxes around geographies. Using such a structure we can describe overlapping hierarchies of locations. For example, we can represent the fact that London is in the UK, and that the postal code SW11

1BD is in Battersea, which is a district in London, which is in southeastern England, which, in turn, is in Great Britain. And because UK postal codes are fine-grained, we can use that boundary to target people with somewhat similar tastes.

 Such pattern-matching queries are extremely difficult to write in SQL, and laborious to write against aggregate stores, and in both cases they tend to perform very poorly. Graph databases, on the other hand, are optimized for precisely these types of traversals and pattern-matching queries, providing in many cases millisecond responses. Moreover, most graph databases provide a query language suited to expressing graph constructs and graph queries. In the next chapter, we'll look at Cypher, which is a pattern-matching language tuned to the way we tend to describe graphs using diagrams.

We can use our example graph to make recommendations to the user, but we can also use it to benefit the seller. For example, given certain buying patterns (products, cost of typical order, and so on), we can establish whether a particular transaction is potentially fraudulent. Patterns outside of the norm for a given user can easily be detected in a graph and be flagged for further attention (using well-known similarity measures from the graph data-mining literature), thus reducing the risk for the seller.

From the data practitioner's point of view, it's clear that the graph database is the best technology for dealing with complex, semi-structured, densely connected data—that is, with datasets so sophisticated they are unwieldy when treated in any form other than a graph.

Summary

In this chapter we've seen how connectedness in relational databases and NOSQL data stores requires developers to implement data processing in the application layer, and contrasted that with graph databases, where connectedness is a first-class citizen. In the next chapter we look in more detail at the topic of graph modeling.

CHAPTER 3

Data Modeling with Graphs

In previous chapters we've described the substantial benefits of the graph database when compared both with document, column family, and key-value NOSQL stores, and with traditional relational databases. But having chosen to adopt a graph database, the question arises: how do we model the world in graph terms?

This chapter focuses on graph modeling. Starting with a recap of the property graph model—the most widely adopted graph data model—we then provide an overview of the graph query language used for most of the code examples in this book: Cypher. Cypher is one of several languages for describing and querying property graphs. There is, as of today, no agreed-upon standard for graph query languages, as exists in the relational database management systems (RDBMS) world with SQL. Cypher was chosen in part because of the authors' fluency with the language, but also because it is easy to learn and understand, and is widely used. With these fundamentals in place, we dive into a couple of examples of graph modeling. With our first example, that of a systems management domain, we compare relational and graph modeling techniques. With the second example, the production and consumption of Shakespearean literature, we use a graph to connect and query several disparate domains. We end the chapter by looking at some common pitfalls when modeling with graphs, and highlight some good practices.

Models and Goals

Before we dig deeper into modeling with graphs, a word on models in general. Modeling is an abstracting activity motivated by a particular need or goal. We model in order to bring specific facets of an unruly domain into a space where they can be structured and manipulated. There are no natural representations of the world the way it "really is," just many purposeful selections, abstractions, and simplifications, some of which are more useful than others for satisfying a particular goal.

Graph representations are no different in this respect. What perhaps differentiates them from many other data modeling techniques, however, is the close affinity between the logical and physical models. Relational data management techniques require us to deviate from our natural language representation of the domain: first by cajoling our representation into a logical model, and then by forcing it into a physical model. These transformations introduce semantic dissonance between our conceptualization of the world and the database's instantiation of that model. With graph databases, this gap shrinks considerably.

We Already Communicate in Graphs

Graph modeling naturally fits with the way we tend to abstract the salient details from a domain using circles and boxes, and then describe the connections between these things by joining them with arrows. Today's graph databases, more than any other database technologies, are "whiteboard friendly." The typical whiteboard view of a problem *is* a graph. What we sketch in our creative and analytical modes maps closely to the data model we implement inside the database. In terms of expressivity, graph databases reduce the impedance mismatch between analysis and implementation that has plagued relational database implementations for many years. What is particularly interesting about such graph models is the fact that they not only communicate how we think things are related, but they also clearly communicate the kinds of questions we want to ask of our domain. As we'll see throughout this chapter, graph models and graph queries are really just two sides of the same coin.

The Property Graph Model

We introduced the property graph model in Chapter 1. To recap, these are its salient features:

- A *property graph* is made up of *nodes*, *relationships*, and *properties.*
- Nodes contain properties. Think of nodes as documents that store properties in the form of arbitrary key-value pairs. The keys are strings and the values are arbitrary data types.
- Relationships connect and structure nodes. A relationship always has a direction, a label, and a *start node* and an *end node*—there are no dangling relationships. Together, a relationship's direction and label add semantic clarity to the structuring of nodes.
- Like nodes, relationships can also have properties. The ability to add properties to relationships is particularly useful for providing additional metadata for graph

algorithms, adding additional semantics to relationships (including quality and weight), and for constraining queries at runtime.

These simple primitives are all we need to create sophisticated and semantically rich models. So far, all our models have been in the form of diagrams. Diagrams are great for describing graphs outside of any technology context, but when it comes to using a database, we need some other mechanism for creating, manipulating, and querying data. We need a query language.

Querying Graphs: An Introduction to Cypher

Cypher is an expressive (yet compact) graph database query language. Although specific to Neo4j, its close affinity with our habit of representing graphs using diagrams makes it ideal for programatically describing graphs in a precise fashion. For this reason, we use Cypher throughout the rest of this book to illustrate graph queries and graph constructions. Cypher is arguably the easiest graph query language to learn, and is a great basis for learning about graphs. Once you understand Cypher, it becomes very easy to branch out and learn other graph query languages.[1]

In the following sections we'll take a brief tour through Cypher. This isn't a reference document for Cypher, however—merely a friendly introduction so that we can explore more interesting graph query scenarios later on.[2]

Other Query Languages

Other graph databases have other means of querying data. Many, including Neo4j, support the RDF query language SPARQL (*http://www.w3.org/TR/rdf-sparql-query/*) and the imperative, path-based query language Gremlin (*https://github.com/tinkerpop/gremlin/wiki/*). Our interest, however, is in the expressive power of a property graph combined with a declarative query language, and so in this book we focus almost exclusively on Cypher.

Cypher Philosophy

Cypher is designed to be easily read and understood by developers, database professionals, and business stakeholders. Its ease of use derives from the fact it accords with the way we intuitively describe graphs using diagrams.

---

1. The Cypher examples in the book were written using Neo4j 2.0. Most of the examples will work with versions 1.8 and 1.9 of Neo4j. Where a particular language feature requires the latest version, we'll point it out.

2. For reference documentation see *http://bit.ly/15Fjjo1* and *http://bit.ly/17l69Mv*.

Cypher enables a user (or an application acting on behalf of a user) to ask the database to find data that matches a specific pattern. Colloquially, we ask the database to "find things like this." And the way we describe what "things like this" look like is to draw them, using ASCII art. Figure 3-1 shows an example of a simple pattern.

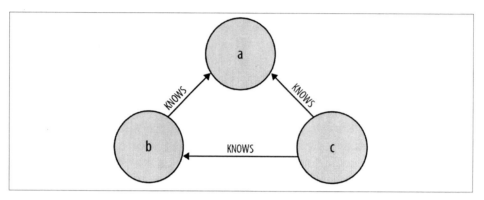

Figure 3-1. A simple graph pattern, expressed using a diagram

This pattern describes three mutual friends. Here's the equivalent ASCII art representation in Cypher:

```
(a)-[:KNOWS]->(b)-[:KNOWS]->(c), (a)-[:KNOWS]->(c)
```

This pattern describes a *path*, which connects a to b, b to c, and a to c. We have to employ a few tricks to get around the fact that a query language has only one dimension (text proceeding from left to right), whereas a graph diagram can be laid out in two dimensions. Here we've had to separate the pattern into two comma-separated subpatterns. But the intent remains clear. On the whole, Cypher patterns follow very naturally from the way we draw graphs on the whiteboard.

Specification By Example

The interesting thing about graph diagrams is that they tend to contain specific instances of nodes and relationships, rather than classes or archetypes. Even very large graphs are typically illustrated using smaller subgraphs made from real nodes and relationships. In other words, we tend to describe graphs using *specification by example*.

ASCII art graph patterns are fundamental to Cypher. A Cypher query anchors one or more parts of a pattern to specific starting locations in a graph, and then flexes the unanchored parts around to find local matches.

The starting locations—the anchor points in the real graph, to which some parts of the pattern are bound—are discovered in one of two ways. The most common method is to use an index. Neo4j uses indexes as naming services; that is, as ways of finding starting locations based on one or more indexed property values.

Like most query languages, Cypher is composed of clauses. The simplest queries consist of a START clause followed by a MATCH and a RETURN clause (we'll describe the other clauses you can use in a Cypher query later in this chapter). Here's an example of a Cypher query that uses these three clauses to find the mutual friends of user named *Michael*:

```
START a=node:user(name='Michael')
MATCH (a)-[:KNOWS]->(b)-[:KNOWS]->(c), (a)-[:KNOWS]->(c)
RETURN b, c
```

Let's look at each clause in more detail.

START

START specifies one or more starting points—nodes or relationships—in the graph. These starting points are obtained via index lookups or, more rarely, accessed directly based on node or relationship IDs.

In the example query, we're looking up a start node in an index called user. We ask the index to find a node with a name property whose value is *Michael*. The return value from this lookup is bound to an *identifier*, which we've here called a. This identifier allows us to refer to this starting node throughout the rest of the query.

MATCH

This is the *specification by example* part. Using ASCII characters to represent nodes and relationships, we *draw* the data we're interested in. We use parentheses to draw nodes, and pairs of dashes and greater-than and less-than signs to draw relationships (- -> and <- -). The < and > signs indicate relationship direction. Between the dashes, set off by square brackets and prefixed by a colon, we put the relationship name.

At the heart of our example query is the simple pattern (a)-[:KNOWS]->(b)-[:KNOWS]->(c), (a)-[:KNOWS]->(c). This pattern describes a path comprising three nodes, one of which we've bound to the identifier a, the others to b and c. These nodes are connected by way of several KNOWS relationships, as per Figure 3-1.

This pattern could, in theory, occur many times throughout our graph data; with a large user set, there may be many mutual relationships corresponding to this pattern. To localize the query, we need to anchor some part of it to one or more places in the graph.

What we've done with the START clause is look up a real node in the graph—the node representing Michael. We bind this Michael node to the a identifier; a then carries over to the MATCH clause. This has the effect of anchoring our pattern to a specific point in the graph. Cypher then matches the remainder of the pattern to the graph immediately surrounding the anchor point. As it does so, it discovers nodes to bind to the other identifiers. While a will always be anchored to Michael, b and c will be bound to a sequence of nodes as the query executes.

RETURN

This clause specifies which nodes, relationships, and properties in the matched data should be returned to the client. In our example query, we're interested in returning the nodes bound to the b and c identifiers. Each matching node is lazily bound to its identifier as the client iterates the results.

Other Cypher Clauses

The other clauses we can use in a Cypher query include:

WHERE
    Provides criteria for filtering pattern matching results.

CREATE *and* CREATE UNIQUE
    Create nodes and relationships.

DELETE
    Removes nodes, relationships, and properties.

SET
    Sets property values.

FOREACH
    Performs an updating action for each element in a list.

UNION
    Merges results from two or more queries (introduced in Neo4j 2.0).

WITH
    Chains subsequent query parts and forward results from one to the next. Similar to piping commands in Unix.

If these clauses look familiar—especially if you're a SQL developer—that's great! Cypher is intended to be familiar enough to help you move rapidly along the learning curve. At the same time, it's different enough to emphasize that we're dealing with graphs, *not* relational sets.

We'll see some examples of these clauses later in the chapter. Where they occur, we'll describe in more detail how they work.

Now that we've seen how we can describe and query a graph using Cypher, we can look at some examples of graph modeling.

A Comparison of Relational and Graph Modeling

To introduce graph modeling, we're going to look at how we model a domain using both relational- and graph-based techniques. Most developers and data professionals are familiar with RDBMS systems and the associated data modeling techniques; as a result, the comparison will highlight a few similarities, and many differences. In particular, we'll see how easy it is to move from a conceptual graph model to a physical graph model, and how little the graph model distorts what we're trying to represent versus the relational model.

To facilitate this comparison, we'll examine a simple data center management domain. In this domain, several data centers support many applications on behalf of many customers using different pieces of infrastructure, from virtual machines to physical load balancers. An example of this domain is shown in Figure 3-2.

In Figure 3-2 we see a somewhat simplified view of several applications and the data center infrastructure necessary to support them. The applications, represented by nodes App 1, App 2, and App 3, depend on a cluster of databases labeled Database Server 1, 2, 3. While users logically depend on the availability of an application and its data, there is additional physical infrastructure between the users and the application; this infrastructure includes virtual machines (Virtual Machine 10, 11, 20, 30, 31), real servers (Server 1, 2, 3), racks for the servers (Rack 1, 2), and load balancers (Load Balancer 1, 2), which front the apps. In between each of the components there are, of course, many networking elements: cables, switches, patch panels, NICs, power supplies, air conditioning, and so on—all of which can fail at inconvenient times. To complete the picture we have a straw-man single user of application 3, represented by User 3.

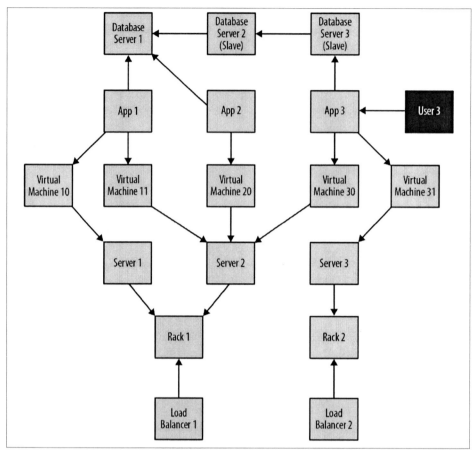

Figure 3-2. Simplified snapshot of application deployment within a data center

As the operators of such a system, we have two primary concerns:

- Ongoing provision of functionality to meet (or exceed) a service-level agreement, including the ability to perform forward-looking analyses to determine single points of failure, and retrospective analyses to rapidly determine the cause of any customer complaints regarding the availability of service.

- Billing for resources consumed, including the cost of hardware, virtualization, network provision, and even the costs of software development and operations (since these are a simply logical extension of the system we see here).

If we are building a data center management solution, we'll want to ensure that the underlying data model allows us to store and query data in a way that efficiently addresses these primary concerns. We'll also want to be able to update the underlying model as the application portfolio changes, the physical layout of the data center evolves, and virtual machine instances migrate. Given these needs and constraints, let's see how the relational and graph models compare.

Relational Modeling in a Systems Management Domain

The initial stage of modeling in the relational world is similar to the first stage of many other data modeling techniques: that is, we seek to understand and agree on the entities in the domain, how they interrelate, and the rules that govern their state transitions. Most of this tends to be done informally, often through whiteboard sketches and discussions between subject matter experts and systems and data architects. To express our common understanding and agreement, we typically create a diagram such as the one in Figure 3-2, which is a graph.

The next stage captures this agreement in a more rigorous form such as an entity-relationship (E-R) diagram—another graph. This transformation of the conceptual model into a logical model using a more strict notation provides us with a second chance to refine our domain vocabulary so that it can be shared with relational database specialists. (Such approaches aren't always necessary: adept relational users often move directly to table design and normalization without first describing an intermediate E-R diagram.) In our example, we've captured the domain in the E-R diagram shown in Figure 3-3.

 Despite being graphs, E-R diagrams immediately demonstrate the shortcomings of the relational model for capturing a rich domain. Although they allow relationships to be named (something that graph databases fully embrace, but which relational stores do not), E-R diagrams allow only *single, undirected*, named relationships between entities. In this respect, the relational model is a poor fit for real-world domains where relationships between entities are both numerous and semantically rich and diverse.

Having arrived at a suitable logical model, we map it into tables and relations, which are normalized to eliminate data redundancy. In many cases this step can be as simple as transcribing the E-R diagram into a tabular form and then loading those tables via SQL commands into the database. But even the simplest case serves to highlight the idiosyncrasies of the relational model. For example, in Figure 3-4 we see that a great deal of accidental complexity has crept into the model in the form of foreign key constraints (everything annotated [FK]), which support one-to-many relationships, and join tables (e.g., AppDatabase), which support many-to-many relationships—and all this before we've added a single row of real user data. These constraints are model-level metadata that exist simply so that we can make concrete the relations between tables at query time. Yet the presence of this structural data is keenly felt, because it clutters and obscures the domain data with data that serves the database, not the user.

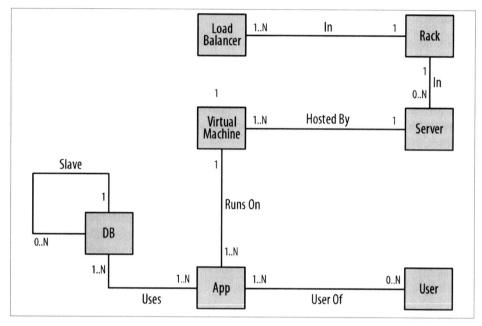

Figure 3-3. An entity-relationship diagram for the data center domain

We now have a normalized model that is relatively faithful to the domain. This model, though imbued with substantial accidental complexity in the form of foreign keys and join tables, contains no duplicate data. But our design work is not yet complete. One of the challenges of the relational paradigm is that normalized models generally aren't fast enough for real-world needs. For many production systems, a normalized schema, which in theory is fit for answering any kind of ad hoc question we may wish to pose to the domain, must in practice be further adapted and specialized for specific access patterns. In other words, to make relational stores perform well enough for regular application needs, we have to abandon any vestiges of true domain affinity and accept that we have to change the user's data model to *suit the database engine, not the user*. This technique is called *denormalization*.

Denormalization involves duplicating data (substantially in some cases) in order to gain query performance. Take as an example users and their contact details. A typical user often has several email addresses, which, in a fully normalized model, we would store in a separate EMAIL table. To reduce joins and the performance penalty imposed by joining between two tables, however, it is quite common to inline this data in the USER table, adding one or more columns to store a user's most important email addresses.

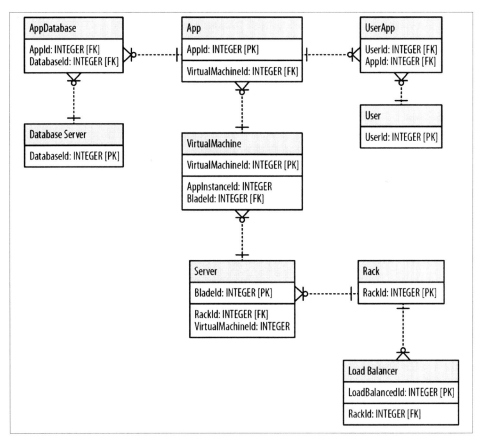

Figure 3-4. Tables and relationships for the data center domain

Although denormalization may be a safe thing to do (assuming developers understand the denormalized model and how it maps to their domain-centric code, *and* have robust transactional support from the database), it is usually not a trivial task. For the best results, we usually turn to a true RDBMS expert to munge our normalized model into a denormalized one aligned with the characteristics of the underlying RDBMS and physical storage tier. In doing this, we accept that there may be substantial data redundancy.

We might be tempted to think that all this design-normalize-denormalize effort is acceptable because it is a one-off task. This school of thought suggests that the cost of the work is amortized across the entire lifetime of the system (which includes both development and production) such that the effort of producing a performant relational model is comparatively small compared to the overall cost of the project. This is an appealing notion, but in many cases it doesn't match reality, because systems change not only during development, but also during their production lifetimes.

The amortized view of data model change, in which costly changes during development are eclipsed by the long-term benefits of a stable model in production, assumes that systems spend the majority of their time in production environments, and that these production environments are stable. Though it may be the case that most systems spend most of their time in production environments, these environments are rarely stable. As business requirements change or regulatory requirements evolve, so must our systems and the data structures on which they are built.

Data models invariably undergo substantial revision during the design and development phases of a project, and in almost every case, these revisions are intended to accommodate the model to the needs of the applications that will consume it once it is in production. These initial design influences are so powerful that it becomes nearly impossible to modify the application and the model once they're in production to accommodate things they were not originally designed to do.

The technical mechanism by which we introduce structural change into a database is called *migration*, as popularized by application development frameworks such as Rails (*http://guides.rubyonrails.org/migrations.html*). Migrations provide a structured, stepwise approach to applying a set of database refactorings (*http://databaserefactoring.com/*) to a database so that it can be responsibly evolved to meet the changing needs of the applications that use it. Unlike code refactorings, however, which we typically accomplish in a matter of seconds or minutes, database refactorings can take weeks or months to complete, with downtime for schema changes. Database refactoring is slow, risky, and expensive.

The problem, then, with the denormalized model is its resistance to the kind of rapid evolution the business demands of its systems. As we've seen with the data center example, the changes imposed on the whiteboard model over the course of implementing a relational solution create a gulf between the conceptual world and the way the data is physically laid out; this conceptual-relational dissonance all but prevents business stakeholders from actively collaborating in the further evolution of a system. Stakeholder participation stops at the threshold of the relational edifice. On the development side, the difficulties in translating changed business requirements into the underlying and entrenched relational structure cause the evolution of the system to lag behind the evolution of the business. Without expert assistance and rigorous planning, migrating a denormalized database poses several risks. If the migrations fail to maintain storage-affinity, performance can suffer. Just as serious, if deliberately duplicated data is left orphaned after a migration, we risk compromising the integrity of the data as a whole.

Graph Modeling in a Systems Management Domain

We've seen how relational modeling and its attendant implementation activities take us down a path that divorces an application's underlying storage model from the conceptual worldview of its stakeholders. Relational databases—with their rigid schemas and complex modeling characteristics—are not an especially good tool for supporting rapid change. What we need is a model that is closely aligned with the domain, but which doesn't sacrifice performance, and which supports evolution while maintaining the integrity of the data as it undergoes rapid change and growth. That model is the graph model. How, then, does this process differ when realized with a graph data model?

In the early stages of analysis, the work required of us is similar to the relational approach: using lo-fi methods such as whiteboard sketches, we describe and agree upon the domain. After that, however, the methodologies diverge. Instead of transforming a domain model's graph-like representation into tables, we enrich it, with the aim of producing an accurate representation of the salient aspects of the domain relevant to what we are trying to achieve in that domain. That is, for each entity in our domain, we ensure that we've captured both the properties and the connections to neighboring entities necessary to support our application goals.

 Remember, the domain model is not a transparent, context-free window onto reality: rather, it is a purposeful abstraction of those aspects of our domain relevant to our application goals. There's always some motivation for creating a model. By enriching our first-cut domain graph with additional properties and relationships, we effectively produce a graph model attuned to our application's data needs; that is, we provide for answering the kinds of questions our application will ask of its data.

Helpfully, domain modeling is completely isomorphic to graph modeling. By ensuring the correctness of the domain model we're implicitly improving the graph model, because in a graph database *what you sketch on the whiteboard is typically what you store in the database.*

In graph terms what we're doing is ensuring each node has the appropriate properties so that it can fulfil its specific data-centric domain responsibilities. But we're also ensuring that every node is in the correct semantic context; we do this by creating named and directed (and often attributed) relationships between the nodes to capture the structural aspects of the domain. For our data center scenario, the resulting graph model looks like Figure 3-5.

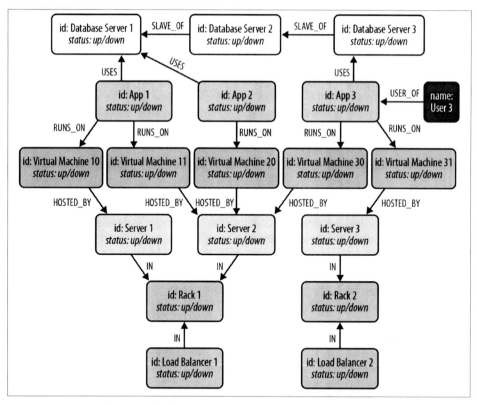

Figure 3-5. Example graph for the data center deployment scenario

And logically, that's *all* we need to do. No tables, no normalization, no denormalization. Once we have an accurate representation of our domain model, moving it into the database is, as we shall see shortly, trivial.

Testing the Model

Once we've refined our domain model, the next step is to test how suitable it is for answering realistic queries. Although graphs are great for supporting a continuously evolving structure (and therefore for correcting any erroneous earlier design decisions), there are a number of design decisions which, once they are baked into our application, can hamper us further down the line. By reviewing the domain model and the resulting graph model at this early stage, we can avoid these pitfalls. Subsequent changes to the graph structure will then be driven solely by changes in the business, rather than by the need to mitigate poor design decisions.

In practice there are two techniques that we can apply here. The first, and simplest, is just to check that the graph reads well. We pick a start node, and then follow relationships to other nodes, reading each node's role and each relationship's name as we go. Doing so should create sensible sentences. For our data center example, we can read off sentences like "Load balancer 1 fronts the App, which consists of App Instance 1, 2, and 3, and the Database, which resides on Database Machine 1 and Database Machine 2," and "Blade 3 runs VM 3, which hosts App Instance 3." If reading the graph in this way makes sense, we can be reasonably confident it is faithful to the domain.

To further increase our confidence, we also need to consider the queries we'll run on the graph. Here we adopt a *design for queryability* mindset. To validate that the graph supports the kinds of queries we expect to run on it, we must describe those queries. This requires us to understand our end users' goals; that is, the use cases to which the graph is to be applied. In our data center scenario, for example, one of our use cases involves end users reporting that an application or service is unresponsive. To help these users, we must identify the cause of the unresponsiveness and then resolve it. To determine what might have gone wrong we need to identify what's on the path between the user and the application, and also what the application depends on to deliver functionality to the user. Given a particular graph representation of the data center domain, if we can craft a Cypher query that addresses this use case, we can be even more certain that the graph meets the needs of our domain.

Continuing with our example use case, let's assume that we can update the graph from our regular network monitoring tools, thereby providing us with a near real-time view of the state of the network. With a large physical network, we might use Complex Event Processing (CEP) (*http://en.wikipedia.org/wiki/Complex_event_processing*) to process streams of low-level network events, updating the graph only when the CEP solution raises a significant domain event. When a user reports a problem, we can limit the physical fault-finding to problematic network elements between the user and the application and the application and its dependencies. In our graph we can find the faulty equipment with the following query:

```
START user=node:users(name = 'User 3')
MATCH (user)-[*1..5]-(asset)
WHERE asset.status! = 'down'
RETURN DISTINCT asset
```

The MATCH clause here describes a *variable length path* between one and five relationships long. The relationships are unnamed and undirected (there's no colon and label between the square brackets, and no greater-than or less-than sign to indicate direction). This allows us to match paths such as:

```
(user)-[:USER_OF]->(app)
(user)-[:USER_OF]->(app)-[:USES]->(database)
(user)-[:USER_OF]->(app)-[:USES]->(database)-[:SLAVE_OF]->(another-database)
(user)-[:USER_OF]->(app)-[:RUNS_ON]->(vm)
(user)-[:USER_OF]->(app)-[:RUNS_ON]->(vm)-[:HOSTED_BY]->(server)
(user)-[:USER_OF]->(app)-[:RUNS_ON]->(vm)-[:HOSTED_BY]->(server)-[:IN]->(rack)
(user)-[:USER_OF]->(app)-[:RUNS_ON]->(vm)-[:HOSTED_BY]->(server)-[:IN]->(rack)
      <-[:IN]-(load-balancer)
```

That is, starting from the user who reported the problem, we MATCH against all assets in the graph along an undirected path of length 1 to 5. We store asset nodes with a sta tus property whose value is 'down' in our results. The exclamation mark in asset.sta tus! ensures that assets that lack a status property are not included in the results. RETURN DISTINCT asset ensures that unique assets are returned in the results, no matter how many times they are matched.

Given that such a query is readily supported by our graph, we gain confidence that the design is fit for purpose.

Cross-Domain Models

Business insight often depends on us understanding the hidden network effects at play in a complex value chain. To generate this understanding, we need to join domains together without distorting or sacrificing the details particular to each domain. Property graphs provide a solution here. Using a property graph, we can model a value chain as a graph of graphs in which specific relationships connect and distinguish constituent subdomains.

In Figure 3-6 we see a graph representation of the value chain surrounding the production and consumption of Shakespearean literature. Here we have high-quality information about Shakespeare and some of his plays, together with details of one of the companies that has recently performed the plays, plus a theatrical venue, and some geospatial data. We've even added a review. In all, the graph describes and connects three different domains. In the diagram we've distinguished these three domains with differently formatted relationships: dotted for the literary domain, solid for the theatrical domain, and dashed for the geospatial domain.

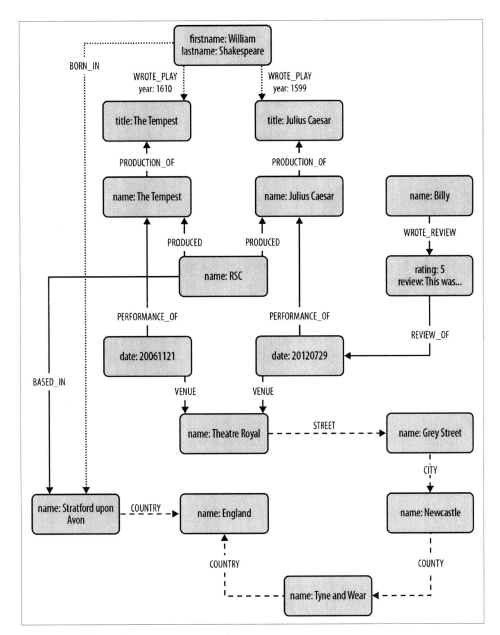

Figure 3-6. Three domains in one graph

Looking first at the literary domain, we have a node that represents Shakespeare himself, with properties firstname: 'William' and lastname: 'Shakespeare'. This node is connected to a pair of nodes representing the plays *Julius Caesar* (title: 'Julius

Caesar') and *The Tempest* (title: 'The Tempest') via relationships labeled WROTE_PLAY.

Reading this subgraph left-to-right, following the direction of the relationship arrows, conveys the fact that *William Shakespeare wrote Julius Caesar and The Tempest*. If we're interested in provenance, each WROTE_PLAY relationship has a date property, which tells us that *Julius Caesar* was written in 1599 and *The Tempest* in 1610. It's a trivial matter to see how we could add the rest of Shakespeare's works—the plays and the poems—into the graph simply by adding more nodes to represent each work, and joining them to the Shakespeare node via WROTE_PLAY and WROTE_POEM relationships.

 By tracing the WROTE_PLAY relationship arrows with our finger, we're effectively doing the kind of work that a graph database performs, albeit at human speed rather than computer speed. As we'll see later, this simple *traversal* operation is the building block for arbitrarily sophisticated graph queries.

Turning next to the theatrical domain, you can see that we've added some information about the Royal Shakespeare Company (often known simply as the *RSC*) in the form of a node with the key company and value RSC. The theatrical domain is, unsurprisingly, connected to the literary domain: in our graph, this is reflected by the fact that the RSC has PRODUCED versions of *Julius Caesar* and *The Tempest*; these theatrical productions are in turn connected to their literary source, the plays in the literary domain using PRODUCTION_OF relationships. The graph also captures details of specific performances: the RSC's production of *Julius Caesar*, for example, was performed on 29 July 2012 as part of the RSC's summer touring season. If we're interested in the performance venue, we simply follow the outgoing VENUE relationship from the performance node to find that the play was performed at the Theatre Royal.

The graph also allows us to capture reviews of specific performances. In our sample graph we've included just one review, for the 29 July performance, written by the user Billy. We can see this in the interplay of the performance, rating, and user nodes. In this case we have a node representing Billy (name: 'Billy') whose outgoing WROTE_RE VIEW relationship connects to a node representing his review. The review node contains a numeric rating property and a free-text review property. The review is linked to a specific performance through an outgoing REVIEW_OF relationship. To scale this up to many users, many reviews, and many performances, we simply add more nodes and more identically named relationships to the graph.

The third domain, that of geospatial data, comprises a simple hierarchical tree of places. This geospatial domain is connected to the other two domains at several points in the graph. The town of Stratford upon Avon (with property name: 'Stratford upon

Avon') is connected to the literary domain as a result of its being Shakespeare's birthplace (Shakespeare was BORN_IN Stratford). It is connected to the theatrical domain insofar as it is home to the RSC (the RSC is BASED_IN Stratford). To learn more about Stratford upon Avon's geography, we can follow its outgoing COUNTRY relationship to discover it is in England.

 Note how the graph reduces instances of duplicated data across domains. *Stratford upon Avon*, for example, participates in all three domains.

The property graph makes it possible to capture more complex geospatial data. Looking at the Theatre Royal, for example, we see that it is located on Grey Street, which is in the CITY of Newcastle, which is in the COUNTY of Tyne and Wear, which ultimately is in the COUNTRY of England—just like Stratford upon Avon.

Relationships help both partition a graph into separate domains *and* connect those domains. As we can see from this relatively simple example, the property graph model makes it easy to unite different domains—each with its own particular entities, properties, and relationships—in a way that not only makes each domain accessible, but also generates insight from the connections between domains.

Labeling Nodes

We've used relationships here to structure the graph and establish the semantic context for each node. By following an outgoing WROTE_REVIEW relationship, for example, we understand that the node at the end of that relationship represents a review. But this is a rather weak method for indicating what kind of domain abstraction a node represents. How might we improve it?

Today, to satisfy this need, many users of Neo4j add type or label properties to their nodes. This is an ad hoc solution to the problem, with no direct support at the level of the query languages and APIs. Forthcoming releases of Neo4j, however, will present users with an enhanced property graph that incorporates labels as first-class citizens of the data model. Labelling allows us to attach one or more labels to a node; using these labels we can then determine which roles or functions a node fulfills. On top of that, we'll be able to ask the graph to find nodes labeled User, or Customer, or even nodes labeled both User *and* Customer. Subsequent releases will allow us to associate constraints with labels, further enhancing our ability to represent and reason about our domain. The first release of the enhanced data model is scheduled to occur around the time this book goes to press.

Creating the Shakespeare Graph

To create the Shakespeare graph shown in Figure 3-6, we use CREATE to build the overall structure. This statement is executed by the Cypher runtime within a single transaction such that once the statement has executed, we can be confident the graph is present in its entirety in the database. If the transaction fails, no part of the graph will be present in the database. As we might expect, Cypher has a humane and visual way of building graphs:

```
CREATE (shakespeare { firstname: 'William', lastname: 'Shakespeare' }),
       (juliusCaesar { title: 'Julius Caesar' }),
       (shakespeare)-[:WROTE_PLAY { year: 1599 }]->(juliusCaesar),
       (theTempest { title: 'The Tempest' }),
       (shakespeare)-[:WROTE_PLAY { year: 1610}]->(theTempest),
       (rsc { name: 'RSC' }),
       (production1 { name: 'Julius Caesar' }),
       (rsc)-[:PRODUCED]->(production1),
       (production1)-[:PRODUCTION_OF]->(juliusCaesar),
       (performance1 { date: 20120729 }),
       (performance1)-[:PERFORMANCE_OF]->(production1),
       (production2 { name: 'The Tempest' }),
       (rsc)-[:PRODUCED]->(production2),
       (production2)-[:PRODUCTION_OF]->(theTempest),
       (performance2 { date: 20061121 }),
       (performance2)-[:PERFORMANCE_OF]->(production2),
       (performance3 { date: 20120730 }),
       (performance3)-[:PERFORMANCE_OF]->(production1),
       (billy { name: 'Billy' }),
       (review { rating: 5, review: 'This was awesome!' }),
       (billy)-[:WROTE_REVIEW]->(review),
       (review)-[:RATED]->(performance1),
       (theatreRoyal { name: 'Theatre Royal' }),
       (performance1)-[:VENUE]->(theatreRoyal),
       (performance2)-[:VENUE]->(theatreRoyal),
       (performance3)-[:VENUE]->(theatreRoyal),
       (greyStreet { name: 'Grey Street' }),
       (theatreRoyal)-[:STREET]->(greyStreet),
       (newcastle { name: 'Newcastle' }),
       (greyStreet)-[:CITY]->(newcastle),
       (tyneAndWear { name: 'Tyne and Wear' }),
       (newcastle)-[:COUNTY]->(tyneAndWear),
       (england { name: 'England' }),
       (tyneAndWear)-[:COUNTRY]->(england),
       (stratford { name: 'Stratford upon Avon' }),
       (stratford)-[:COUNTRY]->(england),
       (rsc)-[:BASED_IN]->(stratford),
       (shakespeare)-[:BORN_IN]->stratford
```

The preceding Cypher code does two different things: it creates nodes (and their properties), and relates nodes (with relationship properties where necessary). For example, CREATE (shakespeare { firstname: 'William', lastname: 'Shakespeare', _la `bel: 'author' })` creates a node representing William Shakespeare. The newly created node is assigned to the identifier `shakespeare`. Identifiers remain available for the duration of the current scope, but no longer; should we wish to give long-lived names to nodes (or relationships), we simply add them to an index. This `shakespeare` identifier is used later in the code to attach relationships to the underlying node. For example, `(shakespeare)-[:WROTE_PLAY { year: 1599 }]->(juliusCaesar)` creates a `WROTE` relationship *from* Shakespeare *to* the play *Julius Caesar*. This relationship has a `year` property with value 1599.

 Unlike the relational model, these commands don't introduce any accidental complexity into the graph. The information meta-model—that is, the structuring of nodes through relationships—is kept separate from the business data, which lives exclusively as properties. We no longer have to worry about foreign key and cardinality constraints polluting our real data, because both are explicit in the graph model in the form of nodes and the semantically rich relationships that interconnect them.

We can modify the graph at a later point in time in two different ways. We can, of course, continue using `CREATE` statements to simply add to the graph. But we can also use `CREATE UNIQUE`, which has the semantics of *ensuring* that a particular subgraph structure—some of which may already exist, some of which may be missing—is in place once the command has executed. In practice, we tend to use `CREATE` when we're adding to the graph and don't mind duplication, and `CREATE UNIQUE` when duplication is not permitted by the domain.

Beginning a Query

Now that we have a graph, we can start to query it. In Cypher we always begin our queries from one or more well-known starting points in the graph—what are called *bound* nodes. (We can also start a query by binding to one or more relationships, but this happens far less frequently than binding to nodes.) This is the purpose of the `START` clause: to give us some starting points, usually drawn from underlying indexes, for exploring the rest of the graph.

For instance, if we wanted to discover more about performances at the Theatre Royal, we'd use the Theatre Royal node as our starting point. However, if we were more interested in a person's reviews, we'd use that person's node as a starting point instead.

Let's assume we want to find out about all the Shakespeare events that have taken place in the Theatre Royal in Newcastle. These three things—Shakespeare, Theatre Royal, and Newcastle—provide the starting points for our new query:

```
START theater=node:venue(name='Theatre Royal'),
      newcastle=node:city(name='Newcastle'),
      bard=node:author(lastname='Shakespeare')
```

This START clause identifies all nodes with a property key name and property value Theatre Royal in a node index called venues. The results of this index lookup are bound to the identifier theater. (What if there are many Theatre Royal nodes in this index? We'll deal with that shortly.) In a second index lookup, we find the node representing the city of Newcastle; we bind this node to the identifier newcastle. Finally, as with our earlier Shakespeare query, to find the Shakespeare node itself, we look in the authors index for a node with a lastname property whose value is Shakespeare. We bind the result of this lookup to bard.

From now on in our query, wherever we use the identifiers theater, newcastle, and bard in a pattern, that pattern will be anchored to the real nodes associated with these identifiers. In effect, the START clause localizes the query, giving us starting points from which to match patterns in the surrounding nodes and relationships.

Declaring Information Patterns to Find

The MATCH clause in Cypher is where the magic happens. Much as the CREATE clause tries to convey intent using ASCII art to describe the desired state of the graph, so the MATCH clause uses the same syntax to describe patterns to discover in the database. We've already looked at a very simple MATCH clause; now we'll look at a more complex pattern that finds all the Shakespeare performances at Newcastle's Theatre Royal:

```
MATCH (newcastle)<-[:STREET|CITY*1..2]-(theater)
      <-[:VENUE]-()-[:PERFORMANCE_OF]->()-[:PRODUCTION_OF]->
      (play)<-[:WROTE_PLAY]-(bard)
```

This MATCH pattern uses several syntactic elements we've not yet come across. As well as including bound nodes based on index lookups (discussed earlier), it uses pattern nodes, arbitrary depth paths, and anonymous nodes. Let's take a look at these in turn:

- The identifiers newcastle, theater, and bard carry over from the START clause, where they were bound to nodes in the graph using index lookups, as described previously.

- If there are several Theatre Royals in our database (the cities of Plymouth, Bath, Winchester, and Norwich all have a Theatre Royal, for example), then theater will be bound to all these nodes. To restrict our pattern to the Theatre Royal in New-castle, we use the syntax <-[:STREET|CITY*1..2]-, which means the theater node can be no more than two outgoing STREET and/or CITY relationships away from the node representing the city of Newcastle. By providing a variable depth path, we allow for relatively fine-grained address hierarchies (comprising, for example, street, district or borough, and city).

- The syntax (theater)<-[:VENUE]-() uses the *anonymous* node, hence the empty parentheses. Knowing the data as we do, we expect the anonymous node to match performances, but because we're not interested in using the details of individual performances elsewhere in the query or in the results, we don't name the node or bind it to an identifier.

- We use the anonymous node again to link the performance to the production (()-[:PERFORMANCE_OF]->()). If we were interested in returning details of performances and productions, we would replace these occurrences of the anonymous node with identifiers: (performance)-[:PERFORMANCE_OF]->(production).

- The remainder of the MATCH is a straightforward (play)<-[:WROTE_PLAY]-(bard) node-to-relationship-to-node pattern match. This pattern ensures we only return plays written by Shakespeare. Because (play) is joined to the anonymous production node, and by way of that to the performance node, we can safely infer that it has been performed in Newcastle's Theatre Royal. In naming the play node we bring it into scope so that we can use it later in the query.

At this point our query looks like this:

```
START theater=node:venue(name='Theatre Royal'),
      newcastle=node:city(name='Newcastle'),
      bard=node:author(lastname='Shakespeare')
MATCH (newcastle)<-[:STREET|CITY*1..2]-(theater)
      <-[:VENUE]-()-[:PERFORMANCE_OF]->()-[:PRODUCTION_OF]->
      (play)<-[:WROTE_PLAY]-(bard)
RETURN DISTINCT play.title AS play
```

Running this query yields all the Shakespeare plays that have been performed at the Theatre Royal in Newcastle:

```
+-----------------+
| play            |
+-----------------+
| "Julius Caesar" |
| "The Tempest"   |
+-----------------+
2 rows
```

That's great if we're interested in the entire history of Shakespeare at the Theatre Royal, but if we're interested only in specific plays, productions, or performances, we need somehow to constrain the set of results.

Constraining Matches

We constrain graph matches using the WHERE clause. WHERE allows us to eliminate matched subgraphs from the results, by stipulating one or more of the following:

- That certain paths must be present (or absent) in the matched subgraphs.

- That specific properties on matched nodes and relationships must be present (or absent), irrespective of their values.
- That certain properties on matched nodes and relationships must have specific values.
- That other arbitrarily complex expression predicates must be met.

Compared to the MATCH clause, which describes structural relationships and assigns identifiers to parts of the pattern, WHERE is more of a tuning exercise to filter down the current pattern match. Let's imagine, for example, that we want to restrict the range of plays in our results to those from Shakespeare's *final period*, which is generally accepted to have begun around 1608. We do this by filtering on the year property of matched WROTE_PLAY relationships. To enable this filtering, we adjust the MATCH clause, binding the WROTE_PLAY relationship to an identifier, which we'll call w. Relationship identifiers come before the colon that prefixes a relationship's name. We then add a WHERE clause that filters on this relationship's year property:

```
START theater=node:venue(name='Theatre Royal'),
      newcastle=node:city(name='Newcastle'),
      bard=node:author(lastname='Shakespeare')
MATCH (newcastle)<-[:STREET|CITY*1..2]-(theater)
      <-[:VENUE]-()-[:PERFORMANCE_OF]->()-[:PRODUCTION_OF]->
      (play)<-[w:WROTE_PLAY]-(bard)
WHERE w.year > 1608
RETURN DISTINCT play.title AS play
```

Adding this WHERE clause means that for each successful match, the Cypher execution engine checks that the WROTE_PLAY relationship between the Shakespeare node and the matched play has a year property with a value greater than 1608. Matches with a WROTE_PLAY relationship whose year value is greater than 1608 will pass the test; these plays will then be included in the results. Matches that fail the test will not be included in the results. By adding this clause, we ensure that only plays from Shakespeare's late period are returned:

```
+---------------+
| play          |
+---------------+
| "The Tempest" |
+---------------+
1 row
```

Processing Results

Cypher's RETURN clause allows us to perform some processing on the matched graph data before returning it to the user (or the application) that executed the query.

As we've seen in the previous queries, the simplest thing we can do is return the plays we've found:

```
RETURN DISTINCT play.title AS play
```

DISTINCT ensures we return unique results. Because each play can be performed multiple times in the same theater, sometimes in different productions, we can end up with duplicate play titles. DISTINCT filters these out.

We can enrich this result in several ways, including aggregating, ordering, filtering, and limiting the returned data. For example, if we're only interested in the *number* of plays that match our criteria, we apply the count function:

```
RETURN count(play)
```

If we want to rank the plays by the number of performances, we'll need first to bind the PERFORMANCE_OF relationship in the MATCH clause to an identifier, called p, which we can then count and order:

```
START theater=node:venue(name='Theatre Royal'),
      newcastle=node:city(name='Newcastle'),
      bard=node:author(lastname='Shakespeare')
MATCH (newcastle)<-[:STREET|CITY*1..2]-(theater)
      <-[:VENUE]-()-[p:PERFORMANCE_OF]->()-[:PRODUCTION_OF]->
      (play)<-[:WROTE_PLAY]-(bard)
RETURN   play.title AS play, count(p) AS performance_count
ORDER BY performance_count DESC
```

The RETURN clause here counts the number of PERFORMANCE_OF relationships using the identifier p (which is bound to the PERFORMANCE_OF relationships in the MATCH clause) and aliases the result as performance_count. It then orders the results based on per formance_count, with the most frequently performed play listed first:

```
+-----------------------------------+
| play            | performance_count |
+-----------------------------------+
| "Julius Caesar" | 2                 |
| "The Tempest"   | 1                 |
+-----------------------------------+
2 rows
```

Query Chaining

Before we leave our brief tour of Cypher, there is one more feature that it is useful to know about—the WITH clause. Sometimes it's just not practical (or possible) to do everything you want in a single MATCH. The WITH clause allows us to chain together several matches, with the results of the previous query part being piped into the next. In the following example we find the plays written by Shakespeare, and order them based on the year in which they were written, latest first. Using `WITH`, we then pipe the results to the `collect` function, which produces a comma-delimited list of play titles:

```
START bard=node:author(lastname='Shakespeare')
MATCH (bard)-[w:WROTE_PLAY]->(play)
WITH play
ORDER BY w.year DESC
RETURN collect(play.title) AS plays
```

Executing this query against our sample graph produces the following result:

```
+---------------------------------+
| plays                           |
+---------------------------------+
| ["The Tempest","Julius Caesar"] |
+---------------------------------+
1 row
```

As queries become more complex, `WITH` instills a sense of discipline, in large part because it insists on separating read-only clauses from write-centric `SET` operations.

Common Modeling Pitfalls

Although graph modeling is a very expressive way of mastering the complexity in a problem domain, expressivity in and of itself is no guarantee that a particular graph is fit for purpose. In fact, there have been occasions where even those of us who work with graphs all the time make mistakes. In this section we'll take a look at a model that went wrong. In so doing, we'll learn how to identify problems early in the modeling effort, and how to fix them.

Email Provenance Problem Domain

This example involves the analysis of email communications. Communication pattern analysis is a classic graph problem. Normally, we'd interrogate the graph to discover subject matter experts, key influencers, and the communication chains through which information is propagated. On this occasion, however, instead of looking for positive role models (in the form of experts), we were searching for rogues: that is, suspicious patterns of email communication that fall foul of corporate governance—or even break the law.

A Sensible First Iteration?

In analyzing the domain we learned about all the clever patterns that potential wrong-doers adopt to cover their tracks: using blind-copying (BCC), using aliases—even conducting conversations with those aliases to mimic legitimate interactions between real business stakeholders. Based on this analysis we produced a representative graph model that seemed to capture all the relevant entities and their activities.

To illustrate this early model, we'll use Cypher's CREATE clause to generate some nodes representing users and aliases. We'll also generate a relationship that shows that Alice is one of Bob's known aliases. (We'll assume that the underlying graph database is indexing these nodes so that we can later look them up and use them as starting points in our queries.) Here's the Cypher query to create our first graph:

```
CREATE (alice {username: 'Alice'}),
       (bob {username: 'Bob'}),
       (charlie {username: 'Charlie'}),
       (davina {username: 'Davina'}),
       (edward {username: 'Edward'}),
       (alice)-[:ALIAS_OF]->(bob)
```

The resulting graph model makes it easy to observe that *Alice is an alias of Bob*, as we see in Figure 3-7.

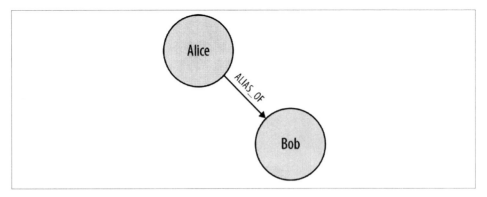

Figure 3-7. Users and aliases

Now we join the users together through the emails they've exchanged:

```
START  bob=node:user(username='Bob'),
       charlie=node:user(username='Charlie'),
       davina=node:user(username='Davina'),
       edward=node:user(username='Edward')
CREATE (bob)-[:EMAILED]->(charlie),
       (bob)-[:CC]->(davina),
       (bob)-[:BCC]->(edward)
```

At first sight this looks like a reasonably faithful representation of the domain. Each clause lends itself to being read comfortably left to right, thereby passing one of our informal tests for correctness. For example, it's deceptively easy to read the sentence "Bob emailed Charlie." The limitations of this model only emerge when it becomes necessary to determine exactly *what* was exchanged by the potential miscreant Bob (and his alter-ego Alice). We can see that Bob CC'd or BCC'd some people, but we can't see the most important thing of all: the email itself.

This first modeling attempt results in a star-shaped graph. Bob is represented by a central node; his actions of emailing, copying, and blind-copying are represented by relationships that extend from Bob to the nodes representing the recipients of his mail. As we see in Figure 3-8, however, the most critical element of the data, the actual *email*, is missing.

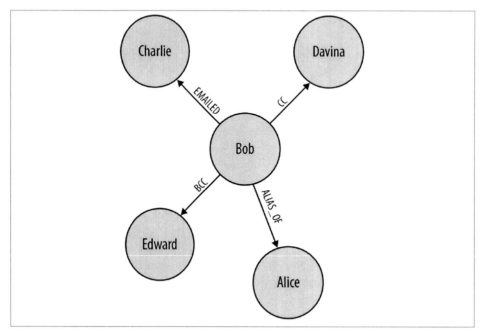

Figure 3-8. Missing email node leads to lost information

That such a structure is lossy becomes evident when we pose the following query:

```
START bob=node:user(username='Bob'),
      charlie=node:user(username='Charlie')
MATCH (bob)-[e:EMAILED]->(charlie)
RETURN e
```

This query returns the EMAILED relationships between Bob and Charlie (there will be one for each email that Bob has sent to Charlie). This tells us that emails have been exchanged, but it tells us nothing about the emails themselves:

```
+----------------+
| e              |
+----------------+
| :EMAILED[1] {} |
+----------------+
1 row
```

We might think we can remedy the situation by adding properties to the EMAILED relationship to represent an email's attributes, but that's just playing for time. Even with properties attached to each EMAILED relationship, we would still be unable to correlate between the EMAILED, CC, and BCC relationships; that is, we would be unable to say which emails were copied versus which were blind-copied, and to whom.

The fact is we've unwittingly made a simple modeling mistake, caused mostly by a lax use of English rather than any shortcomings of graph theory. Our everyday use of language has lead us to focus on the verb "emailed" rather than the email itself, and as a result we've produced a model lacking domain insight.

In English, it's easy and convenient to shorten the phrase "Bob sent an email to Charlie" to "Bob emailed Charlie". In most cases that loss of a noun (the actual email) doesn't matter because the intent is still clear. But when it comes to our forensics scenario, these elided statements are problematic. The intent remains the same, but the details of the number, contents, and recipients of the emails that Bob sent have been lost through having been folded into a relationship EMAILED, rather than being modeled explicitly as nodes in their own right.

Second Time's the Charm

To fix our lossy model, we need to insert email nodes to represent the real emails exchanged within the business, and expand our set of relationship names to encompass the full set of addressing fields that email supports. Now instead of creating lossy structures like this:

```
CREATE (bob)-[:EMAILED]->(charlie)
```

we'll instead create more detailed structures, like this:

```
CREATE (email_1 {id: '1', content: 'Hi Charlie, ... Kind regards, Bob'}),
       (bob)-[:SENT]->(email_1),
       (email_1)-[:TO]->(charlie),
       (email_1)-[:CC]->(davina),
       (email_1)-[:CC]->(alice),
       (email_1)-[:BCC]->(edward)
```

This results in the kind of graph structure we see in Figure 3-9.

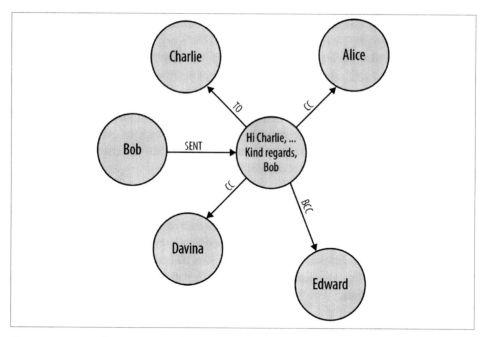

Figure 3-9. Introducing an email node produces a star graph

Of course, in a real system there will be many more of these emails, each with its intricate web of interactions for us to explore. It's quite easy to imagine that over time many more CREATE statements are executed as the email server logs the interactions, like so (we've omitted the START clauses for brevity):

```
CREATE (email_1 {id: '1', content: 'email contents'}),
       (bob)-[:SENT]->(email_1),
       (email_1)-[:TO]->(charlie),
       (email_1)-[:CC]->(davina),
       (email_1)-[:CC]->(alice),
       (email_1)-[:BCC]->(edward);

CREATE (email_2 {id: '2', content: 'email contents'}),
       (bob)-[:SENT]->(email_2),
       (email_2)-[:TO]->(davina),
       (email_2)-[:BCC]->(edward);

CREATE (email_3 {id: '3', content: 'email contents'}),
       (davina)-[:SENT]->(email_3),
       (email_3)-[:TO]->(bob),
       (email_3)-[:CC]->(edward);

CREATE (email_4 {id: '4', content: 'email contents'}),
       (charlie)-[:SENT]->(email_4),
       (email_4)-[:TO]->(bob),
```

```
        (email_4)-[:TO]->(davina),
        (email_4)-[:TO]->(edward);

CREATE (email_5 {id: '5', content: 'email contents'}),
        (davina)-[:SENT]->(email_5),
        (email_5)-[:TO]->(alice),
        (email_5)-[:BCC]->(bob),
        (email_5)-[:BCC]->(edward);
```

This leads to the more complex, and interesting, graph we see in Figure 3-10.

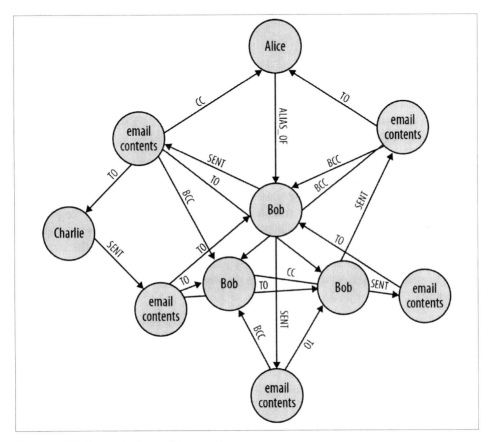

Figure 3-10. A graph of email interactions

We can now query this graph to identify potentially suspect behavior:

```
START bob=node:user(username='Bob')
MATCH (bob)-[:SENT]->(email)-[:CC]->(alias),
      (alias)-[:ALIAS_OF]->(bob)
RETURN email
```

Here we retrieve all the emails that Bob has sent where he's CC'd one of his own aliases. Any emails that match this pattern are indicative of rogue behavior. And because both Cypher and the underlying graph database have graph affinity, these queries—even over large datasets—run very quickly. This query returns the following results:

```
+------------------------------------------+
| email                                    |
+------------------------------------------+
| Node[6]{id:"1",content:"email contents"} |
+------------------------------------------+
1 row
```

Evolving the Domain

As with any database, our graph serves a system that is likely to evolve over time. So what should we do when the graph evolves? How do we know what breaks, or indeed, how do we even tell that something has broken? The fact is, we can't avoid *migrations* in a graph database: they're a fact of life, just as with any data store. But in a graph database they're often simpler.

In a graph, to add new facts or compositions, we tend to add new nodes and relationships rather than changing the model in place. Adding to the graph using *new* kinds of relationships will not affect any existing queries, and is completely safe. Changing the graph using *existing* relationship types, and changing the properties (not just the property values) of existing nodes *might* be safe, but we need to run a representative set of queries to maintain confidence that the graph is still fit for purpose after the the structural changes. However, these activities are precisely the same kinds of actions we perform during normal database operation, so in a graph world a migration really is just business as normal.

At this point we have a graph that describes who sent and received emails, as well as the content of the emails themselves. But of course, one of the joys of email is that recipients can forward or reply to an email they've received. This increases interaction and knowledge sharing, but in some cases leaks critical business information. Given we're looking for suspicious communication patterns, it makes sense for us to also take into account forwarding and replies.

At first glance, there would appear to be no need to use database migrations to update our graph to support our new use case. The simplest additions we can make involve adding FORWARDED and REPLIED_TO relationships to the graph, as shown in Figure 3-11. Doing so won't affect any preexisting queries because they aren't coded to recognize the new relationships.

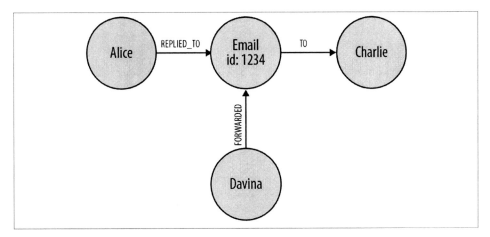

Figure 3-11. A naive, lossy approach fails to appreciate that forwarded and replied-to emails are first-class entities

However, this approach quickly proves inadequate. Adding FORWARDED or REPLIED relationships is naive and lossy in much the same way as our original use of an EMAILED relationship. To illustrate this, consider the following CREATE statements:

```
START email = node:emails(id='1234');
CREATE (alice)-[:REPLIED_TO]->(email);
CREATE (davina)-[:FORWARDED]->(email)-[:TO]->(charlie);
```

In the first CREATE statement we're trying to record the fact that Alice replied to a particular email. The statement makes logical sense when read from left to right, but the sentiment is lossy—we can't tell whether Alice replied to all the recipients of email or directly to the author. All we know is that some reply was sent. The second statement also reads well from left to right: Davina forwarded email to Charlie. But we already use the TO relationship to indicate that a given email has a TO header identifying the primary recipients. Reusing TO here makes it impossible to tell who was a recipient and who received a forwarded version of an email.

To resolve this problem, we have to consider the fundamentals of the domain. A reply to an email is itself a new email, albeit with some relationship to a previous message. Whether the reply is to the original sender, all recipients, or a subset can be easily modeled using the same familiar TO, CC, and BCC relationships, while the original email itself can be referenced via a REPLY_TO relationship. Here's a revised series of writes resulting from several email actions (again, we've omitted the necessary START clauses):

```
CREATE (email_6 {id: '6', content: 'email'}),
       (bob)-[:SENT]->(email_6),
       (email_6)-[:TO]->(charlie),
       (email_6)-[:TO]->(davina);
```

```
CREATE (reply_1 {id: '7', content: 'response'}),
       (reply_1)-[:REPLY_TO]->(email_6),
       (davina)-[:SENT]->(reply_1),
       (reply_1)-[:TO]->(bob),
       (reply_1)-[:TO]->(charlie);

CREATE (reply_2 {id: '8', content: 'response'}),
       (reply_2)-[:REPLY_TO]->(email_6),
       (bob)-[:SENT]->(reply_2),
       (reply_2)-[:TO]->(davina),
       (reply_2)-[:TO]->(charlie),
       (reply_2)-[:CC]->(alice);

CREATE (reply_3 {id: '9', content: 'response'}),
       (reply_3)-[:REPLY_TO]->(reply_1),
       (charlie)-[:SENT]->(reply_3),
       (reply_3)-[:TO]->(bob),
       (reply_3)-[:TO]->(davina);

CREATE (reply_4 {id: '10', content: 'response'}),
       (reply_4)-[:REPLY_TO]->(reply_3),
       (bob)-[:SENT]->(reply_4),
       (reply_4)-[:TO]->(charlie),
       (reply_4)-[:TO]->(davina);
```

This creates the graph in Figure 3-12, which shows numerous replies and replies-to-replies.

Now it is easy to see who replied to Bob's original email. First locate the email of interest, then match against all incoming REPLY_TO relationships (there may be multiple replies), and from there match against incoming SENT relationships: this reveals the sender(s). In Cypher this is simple to express. In fact, Cypher makes it easy to look for replies-to-replies-to-replies, and so on to an arbitrary depth (though we limit it to depth four here):

```
START email = node:email(id = '6')
MATCH p=(email)<-[:REPLY_TO*1..4]-()<-[:SENT]-(replier)
RETURN replier.username AS replier, length(p) - 1 AS depth
ORDER BY depth
```

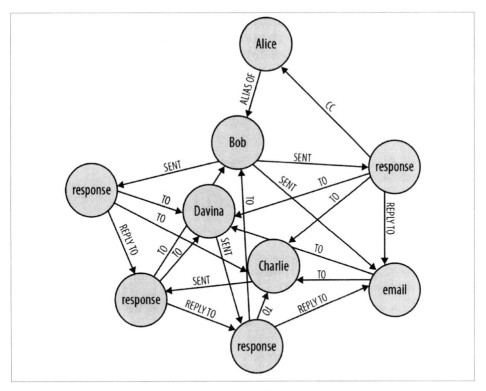

Figure 3-12. Explicitly modeling replies in high-fidelity

Here we capture each matched path, binding it to the identifier p. In the RETURN clause we then calculate the length of the reply-to chain (subtracting 1 for the SENT relationship), and return the replier's name and the depth at which he or she replied. This query returns the following results:

```
+-------------------+
| replier  | depth  |
+-------------------+
| "Davina" | 1      |
| "Bob"    | 1      |
| "Charlie"| 2      |
| "Bob"    | 3      |
+-------------------+
4 rows
```

We see that both Davina and Bob replied directly to Bob's original email; that Charlie replied to one of the replies; and that Bob then replied to one of the replies to a reply.

It's a similar pattern for a forwarded email: a forwarded email is simply a new email that happens to contain some of the text of the original email. In that case we should model the new email explicitly, just as in the reply case. But from an application point of view we should also be able to reference the original email from the forwarded mail so that we always have detailed and accurate provenance data. And the same applies if the forwarded mail is itself forwarded, and so on. For example, if Alice (Bob's alter-ego) emails Bob to try to establish separate concrete identities, and then Bob (wishing to perform some subterfuge) forwards that email onto Charlie, who then forwards it onto Davina, we actually have three emails to consider. Assuming the users (and their aliases) are already in the database, in Cypher we'd write that audit information into the database as follows:

```
CREATE (email_11 {id: '11', content: 'email'}),
       (alice)-[:SENT]->(email_11)-[:TO]->(bob);

CREATE (email_12 {id: '12', content: 'email'}),
       (email_12)-[:FORWARD_OF]->(email_11),
       (bob)-[:SENT]->(email_12)-[:TO]->(charlie);

CREATE (email_13 {id: '13', content: 'email'}),
       (email_13)-[:FORWARD_OF]->(email_12),
       (charlie)-[:SENT]->(email_13)-[:TO]->(davina);
```

On completion of these writes, our database will contain the subgraph shown in Figure 3-13.

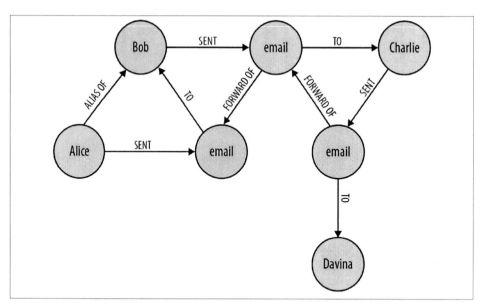

Figure 3-13. Explicitly modeling email forwarding

Using this graph, we can determine the length of an email chain.

```
START email = node:email(id = '11')
MATCH (email)<-[f:FORWARD_OF*]-()
RETURN count(f)
```

This query starts at the given email and then matches against all incoming FOR
WARD_OF relationships to any depth. These relationships are bound to an identifier f. To
calculate the length of the email chain, we count the number of FORWARD_OF relationships
bound to f using Cypher's count function. In this example, we see the original email
has been forwarded twice:

```
+----------+
| count(f) |
+----------+
| 2        |
+----------+
1 row
```

Avoiding Anti-Patterns

In the general case, don't encode entities into relationships. Use relationships to convey
semantics about *how* entities are related, and the quality of those relationships. Domain
entities aren't always immediately visible in speech, so we must think carefully about
the nouns we're actually dealing with.

It's also important to realize that graphs are a naturally additive structure. It's quite
natural to add facts in terms of domain entities and how they interrelate using new
nodes and new relationships, even if it feels like we're flooding the database with a great
deal of painstaking data. In general, it's bad practice to try to conflate data elements at
write time to preserve query-time efficiency. If we model in accordance with the questions we want to ask of our data, an accurate representation of the domain will emerge.
With this data model in place, we can trust the graph database to do the right thing.

 Graph databases maintain fast query times even when storing vast
amounts of data. Learning to trust our graph database is important
when learning to structure our graphs without denormalizing them.

Summary

Graph databases give software professionals the power to represent a problem domain
using a graph, and then persist and query that graph at runtime. We can use graphs to
clearly describe a problem domain; graph databases then allow us to store this representation in a way that maintains high affinity between the domain and the data. Further,
graph modeling removes the need to normalize and denormalize data using complex
data management code.

Many of us, however, will be new to modeling with graphs. The graphs we create should read well for queries, while avoiding conflating entities and actions—bad practices that can lose useful domain knowledge. Although there are no absolute rights or wrongs to graph modeling, the guidance in this chapter will help you create graph data that can serve your systems' needs over many iterations, all the while keeping pace with code evolution.

Armed with an understanding of graph data modeling, you may now be considering undertaking a graph database project. In the next chapter we'll look at what's involved in planning and delivering a graph database solution.

CHAPTER 4

Building a Graph Database Application

In this chapter we discuss some of the practical issues of working with a graph database. In previous chapters we've looked at graph data; in this chapter, we'll apply that knowledge in the context of developing a graph database application. We'll look at some of the data modeling questions that may arise, and at some of the application architecture choices available to us.

In our experience, graph database applications are highly amenable to being developed using the evolutionary, incremental, and iterative software development practices in widespread use today. A key feature of these practices is the prevalence of testing throughout the software development life cycle. Here we'll show how we develop our data model and our application in a test-driven fashion.

At the end of the chapter, we'll look at some of the issues we'll need to consider when planning for production.

Data Modeling

We covered modeling and working with graph data in detail in Chapter 3. Here we summarize some of the more important modeling guidelines, and discuss how implementing a graph data model fits with iterative and incremental software development techniques.

Describe the Model in Terms of the Application's Needs

The *questions* we need to ask of the data help identify entities and relationships. Agile user stories provide a concise means for expressing an outside-in, user-centered view of an application's needs, and the questions that arise in the course of satisfying this need.[1] Here's an example of a user story for a book review web application:

> **AS A** reader who likes a book, **I WANT** to know which books other readers who like the same book have liked, **SO THAT** I can find other books to read.

This story expresses a user need, which motivates the shape and content of our data model. From a data modeling point of view, the AS A clause establishes a context comprising two entities—a reader and a book—plus the LIKES relationship that connects them. The I WANT clause then poses a question: which books have the readers who like the book I'm currently reading also liked? This question exposes more LIKES relationships, and more entities: other readers and other books.

The entities and relationships that we've surfaced in analyzing the user story quickly translate into a simple data model, as shown in Figure 4-1.

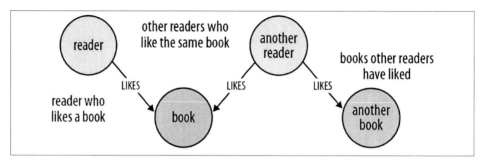

Figure 4-1. Data model for the book reviews user story

Because this data model directly encodes the question presented by the user story, it lends itself to being queried in a way that similarly reflects the structure of the question we want to ask of the data:

```
START reader=node:users(name={readerName})
      book=node:books(isbn={bookISBN})
MATCH reader-[:LIKES]->book<-[:LIKES]-other_readers-[:LIKES]->books
RETURN books.title
```

Nodes for Things, Relationships for Structure

Though not applicable in every situation, these general guidelines will help us choose when to use nodes, and when to use relationships:

---

1. For agile user stories, see Mike Cohn, *User Stories Applied* (Addison-Wesley, 2004).

- Use nodes to represent entities—that is, the *things* that are of interest to us in our domain.

- Use relationships both to express the *connections* between entities and to establish semantic context for each entity, thereby structuring the domain.

- Use relationship direction to further clarify relationship semantics. Many relationships are asymmetrical, which is why relationships in a property graph are always directed. For bidirectional relationships, we should make our queries ignore direction.

- Use node properties to represent entity attributes, plus any necessary entity metadata, such as timestamps, version numbers, etc.

- Use relationship properties to express the strength, weight, or quality of a relationship, plus any necessary relationship metadata, such as timestamps, version numbers, etc.

It pays to be diligent about discovering and capturing domain entities. As we saw in Chapter 3, it's relatively easy to model things that really ought to be represented as nodes using sloppily named relationships instead. If we're tempted to use a relationship to model an entity—an email, or a review, for example—we must make certain that this entity cannot be related to more than two other entities. Remember, a relationship must have a start node and an end node—nothing more, nothing less. If we find later that we need to connect something we've modeled as a relationship to more than two other entities, we'll have to refactor the entity inside the relationship out into a separate node. This is a breaking change to the data model, and will likely require us to make changes to any queries and application code that produce or consume the data.

Fine-Grained versus Generic Relationships

When designing relationship types we should be mindful of the trade-offs between using fine-grained relationship labels versus generic relationships qualified with properties. It's the difference between using DELIVERY_ADDRESS and HOME_ADDRESS versus ADDRESS {type: 'delivery'} and ADDRESS {type: 'home'}.

Relationships are the royal road into the graph. Differentiating by relationship type is the best way of eliminating large swathes of the graph from a traversal. Using one or more property values to decide whether or not to follow a relationship incurs extra IO the first time those properties are accessed because the properties reside in a separate store file from the relationships (after that, however, they're cached).

We use fine-grained relationships whenever we have a closed set of relationship types. In contrast, weightings—as required by a shortest-weighted-path algorithm—rarely comprise a closed set, and these are usually best represented as properties on relationships.

Sometimes, however, we have a closed set of relationships, but in some traversals we want to follow specific kinds of relationships within that set, whereas in others we want to follow all of them, irrespective of type. Addresses are a good example. Following the closed-set principle, we might choose to create HOME_ADDRESS, WORK_ADDRESS, and DE LIVERY_ADDRESS relationships. This allows us to follow specific kinds of address relationships (DELIVERY_ADDRESS, for example) while ignoring all the rest. But what do we do if we want to find *all* addresses for a user? There are a couple of options here. First, we can encode knowledge of all the different relationship types in our queries: e.g., MATCH user-[:HOME_ADDRESS|WORK_ADDRESS|DELIVERY_ADDRESS]->address. This, however, quickly becomes unwieldy when there are lots of different kinds of relationships. Alternatively, we can add a more generic ADDRESS relationship to our model, in addition to the fine-grained relationships. Every node representing an address is then connected to a user using two relationships: a fined-grained relationship (e.g., DELIV ERY_ADDRESS) *and* the more generic ADDRESS {type: 'delivery'} relationship.

As we discussed in "Describe the Model in Terms of the Application's Needs" on page 63, the key here is to let the questions we want to ask of our data guide the kinds of relationships we introduce into the model.

Model Facts as Nodes

When two or more domain entities interact for a period of time, a fact emerges. We represent these facts as separate nodes, with connections to each of the entities engaged in that fact. Modeling an action in terms of its product—that is, in terms of the *thing* that results from the action—produces a similar structure: an intermediate node that represents the outcome of an interaction between two or more entities. We can use timestamp properties on this intermediate node to represent start and end times.

The following examples show how we might model facts and actions using intermediate nodes.

Employment

Figure 4-2 shows how the fact of Ian being employed by Neo Technology in the role of engineer can be represented in the graph.

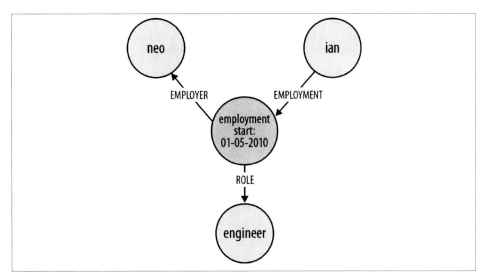

Figure 4-2. Ian was employed as an engineer at Neo Technology

In Cypher, this can be expressed as:

```
(ian)-[:EMPLOYMENT]->(employment)-[:EMPLOYER]->(neo),
(employment)-[:ROLE]->(engineer)
```

Performance

Figure 4-3 shows how the fact of William Hartnell having played the Doctor in the story *The Sensorites* can be represented in the graph.

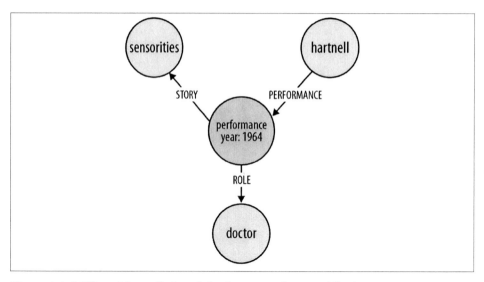

Figure 4-3. William Hartnell played the Doctor in the story The Sensorites

In Cypher:

```
(hartnell)-[:PERFORMANCE]->(performance)-[:ROLE]->(doctor),
(performance)-[:STORY]->(sensorites)
```

Emailing

Figure 4-4 shows the act of Ian emailing Jim and copying in Alistair.

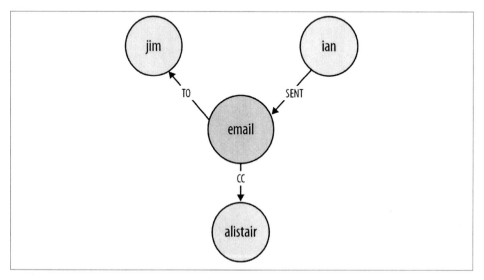

Figure 4-4. Ian emailed Jim, and copied in Alistair

In Cypher, this can be expressed as:

```
(ian)-[:SENT]->(email)-[:TO]->(jim),
(email)-[:CC]->(alistair)
```

Reviewing

Figure 4-5 shows how the act of Alistair reviewing a film can be represented in the graph.

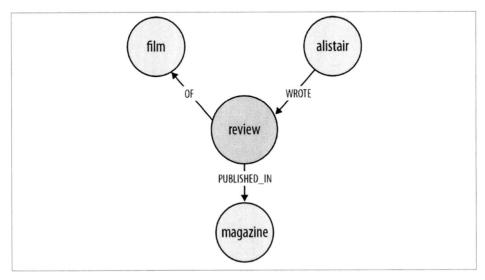

Figure 4-5. Alistair wrote a review of a film, which was published in a magazine

In Cypher:

```
(alistair)-[:WROTE]->(review)-[:OF]->(film),
(review)-[:PUBLISHED_IN]->(magazine)
```

Represent Complex Value Types as Nodes

Value types are things that do not have an identity, and whose equivalence is based solely on their values. Examples include *money, address*, and *SKU*. Complex value types are value types with more than one field or property. *Address*, for example, is a complex value type. Such multiproperty value types are best represented as separate nodes:

```
START ord=node:orders(orderid={orderId})
MATCH (ord)-[:DELIVERY_ADDRESS]->(address)
RETURN address.first_line, address.zipcode
```

Time

Time can be modeled in several different ways in the graph. Here we describe two techniques: timeline trees and linked lists.

Timeline trees

If we need to find all the events that have occurred over a specific period, we can build a timeline tree, as shown in Figure 4-6.

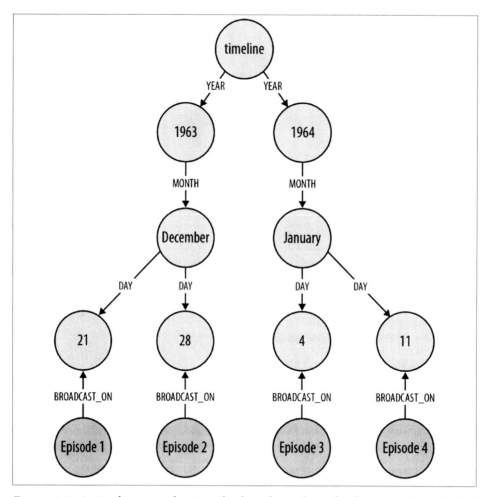

Figure 4-6. A timeline tree showing the broadcast dates for four episodes of a TV program

Each year has its own set of month nodes; each month has its own set of day nodes. We need only insert nodes into the timeline tree as and when they are needed. Assuming the root `timeline` node has been indexed, or is in some other way discoverable, the following Cypher statement will insert all necessary nodes for a particular event—year, month, day, plus the node representing the event to be attached to the timeline:

```
START timeline=node:timeline(name={timelineName})
CREATE UNIQUE (timeline)-[:YEAR]->(year{value:{year}, name:{yearName}})
              -[:MONTH]->(month{value:{month}, name:{monthName}})
              -[:DAY]->(day{value:{day}, name:{dayName}})
              <-[:BROADCAST_ON]-(n {newNode})
```

Querying the calendar for all events between a start date (inclusive) and an end date (exclusive) can be done with the following Cypher:

```
START timeline=node:timeline(name={timelineName})
MATCH (timeline)-[:YEAR]->(year)-[:MONTH]->(month)-[:DAY]->
      (day)<-[:BROADCAST_ON]-(n)
WHERE ((year.value > {startYear} AND year.value < {endYear})
      OR ({startYear} = {endYear} AND {startMonth} = {endMonth}
          AND year.value = {startYear} AND month.value = {startMonth}
          AND day.value >= {startDay} AND day.value < {endDay})
      OR ({startYear} = {endYear} AND {startMonth} < {endMonth}
          AND year.value = {startYear}
          AND ((month.value = {startMonth} AND day.value >= {startDay})
              OR (month.value > {startMonth} AND month.value < {endMonth})
              OR (month.value = {endMonth} AND day.value < {endDay})))
      OR ({startYear} < {endYear}
          AND year.value = {startYear}
          AND ((month.value > {startMonth})
              OR (month.value = {startMonth} AND day.value >= {startDay})))
      OR ({startYear} < {endYear}
          AND year.value = {endYear}
          AND ((month.value < {endMonth})
              OR (month.value = {endMonth} AND day.value < {endDay})))))
RETURN n
```

The `WHERE` clause here, though somewhat verbose, simply filters each match based on the start and end dates supplied to the query.

Linked lists

Many events have temporal relationships to the events that precede and follow them. We can use `NEXT` and `PREVIOUS` relationships (or similar) to create linked lists that capture this natural ordering, as shown in Figure 4-7. Linked lists allow for very rapid traversal of time-ordered events.

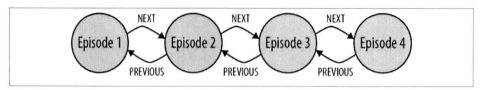

Figure 4-7. A doubly linked list representing a time-ordered series of events

Versioning

A versioned graph enables us to recover the state of the graph at a particular point in time. Most graph databases don't support versioning as a first-class concept: it is possible, however, to create a versioning scheme inside the graph model whereby nodes and relationships are timestamped and archived whenever they are modified.[2] The downside of such versioning schemes is that they leak into any queries written against the graph, adding a layer of complexity to even the simplest query.

Iterative and Incremental Development

We develop the data model feature by feature, user story by user story. This will ensure we identify the relationships our application will use to query the graph. A data model that is developed in line with the iterative and incremental delivery of application features will look quite different from one drawn up using a data model-first approach, but it will be the correct model, motivated throughout by specific needs, and the questions that arise in conjunction with those needs.

Graph databases provide for the smooth evolution of our data model. Migrations and denormalization are rarely an issue. New facts and new compositions become new nodes and relationships, while optimizing for performance-critical access patterns typically involves introducing a direct relationship between two nodes that would otherwise be connected only by way of intermediaries. Unlike the optimization strategies we employ in the relational world, which typically involve denormalizing and thereby compromising a high-fidelity model, this is not an either/or issue: either the detailed, highly normalized structure, or the high performance compromise. With the graph we retain the original high-fidelity graph structure, while at the same time enriching it with new elements that cater to new needs.

We will quickly see how different relationships can sit side-by-side with one another, catering to different needs without distorting the model in favor of any one particular need. Addresses help illustrate the point here. Imagine, for example, that we are developing a retail application. While developing a fulfillment story, we add the ability to

---

2. See, for example, *https://github.com/dmontag/neo4j-versioning*, which uses Neo4j's transaction life cycle to create versioned copies of nodes and relationships.

---

dispatch a parcel to a customer's delivery address, which we find using the following query:

```
START user=node:users(id={userId})
MATCH (user)-[:DELIVERY_ADDRESS]->(address)
RETURN address
```

Later on, when adding some billing functionality, we introduce a BILLING_ADDRESS relationship. Later still, we add the ability for customers to manage all their addresses. This last feature requires us to find all addresses—whether delivery, or billing, or some other address. To facilitate this, we introduce a general ADDRESS relationship:

```
START user=node:users(id={userId})
MATCH (user)-[:ADDRESS]->(address)
RETURN address
```

By this time, our data model looks something like the one shown in Figure 4-8. DELIV ERY_ADDRESS specializes the data on behalf of the application's fulfillment needs; BILL ING_ADDRESS specializes the data on behalf of the application's billing needs; and AD DRESS specializes the data on behalf of the application's customer management needs.

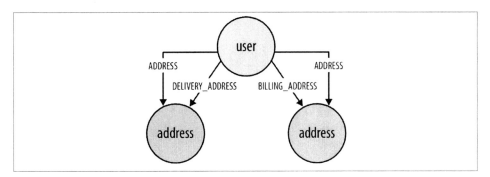

Figure 4-8. Different relationships for different application needs

Being able to add new relationships to meet new application needs doesn't mean we should always do this. We'll invariably identify opportunities for refactoring the model as we go: there'll be plenty of times, for example, where renaming an existing relationship will allow it to be used for two different needs. When these opportunities arise, we should take them. If we're developing our solution in a test-driven manner—described in more detail later in this chapter—we'll have a sound suite of regression tests in place, enabling us to make substantial changes to the model with confidence.

Application Architecture

In planning a graph database-based solution, there are several architectural decisions to be made. These decisions will vary slightly depending on the database product we've chosen; in this section, we'll describe some of the architectural choices, and the corresponding application architectures, available to us when using Neo4j.

Embedded Versus Server

Most databases today run as a server that is accessed through a client library. Neo4j is somewhat unusual in that it can be run in embedded as well as server mode—in fact, going back nearly ten years, its origins are as an embedded graph database.

 An embedded database is not the same as an in-memory database. An embedded instance of Neo4j still makes all data durable on disk. Later, in "Testing" on page 82, we'll discuss ImpermanentGraphDatabase, which is an in-memory version of Neo4j designed for testing purposes.

Embedded Neo4j

In embedded mode, Neo4j runs in the same process as our application. Embedded Neo4j is ideal for hardware devices, desktop applications, and for incorporating in our own application servers. Some of the advantages of embedded mode include:

Low latency
: Because our application speaks directly to the database, there's no network overhead.

Choice of APIs
: We have access to the full range of APIs for creating and querying data: the Core API, traversal framework, and the Cypher query language.

Explicit transactions
: Using the Core API, we can control the transactional life cycle, executing an arbitrarily complex sequence of commands against the database in the context of a single transaction. The Java APIs also expose the transaction life cycle, enabling us to plug in custom transaction event handlers (*http://docs.neo4j.org/chunked/stable/transactions-events.html*) that execute additional logic with each transaction.

Named indexes
: Embedded mode gives us full control over the creation and management of named indexes. This functionality is also available through the web-based REST interface; it is not, however, available in Cypher.

When running in embedded mode, however, we should bear in mind the following:

JVM only
: Neo4j is a JVM-based database. Many of its APIs are, therefore, accessible only from a JVM-based language.

GC behaviors

When running in embedded mode, Neo4j is subject to the garbage collection (GC) behaviors of the host application. Long GC pauses can affect query times. Further, when running an embedded instance as part of an HA cluster, long GC pauses can cause the cluster protocol to trigger a master reelection.

Database life cycle

The application is responsible for controlling the database life cycle, which includes starting it, and closing it safely.

Embedded Neo4j can be clustered for high availability and horizontal read scaling just as the server version. In fact, we can run a mixed cluster of embedded and server instances (clustering is performed at the database level, rather than the server level). This is common in enterprise integration scenarios, where regular updates from other systems are executed against an embedded instance, and then replicated out to server instances.

Server mode

Running Neo4j in server mode is the most common means of deploying the database today. At the heart of each server is an embedded instance of Neo4j. Some of the benefits of server mode include:

REST API

The server exposes a rich REST API that allows clients to send JSON-formatted requests over HTTP. Responses comprise JSON-formatted documents enriched with hypermedia links that advertise additional features of the dataset.

Platform independence

Because access is by way of JSON-formatted documents sent over HTTP, a Neo4j server can be accessed by a client running on practically any platform. All that's needed is an HTTP client library.[3]

Scaling independence

With Neo4j running in server mode, we can scale our database cluster independently of our application server cluster.

Isolation from application GC behaviors

In server mode, Neo4j is protected from any untoward GC behaviors triggered by the rest of the application. Of course, Neo4j still produces some garbage, but its impact on the garbage collector has been carefully monitored and tuned during development to mitigate any significant side effects. However, because server

---

3. A list of Neo4j remote client libraries, as developed by the community, is maintained at *http://bit.ly/YEHRrD*.

extensions enable us to run arbitrary Java code inside the server (see "Server extensions"), the use of server extensions may impact the server's GC behavior.

When using Neo4j in server mode, we should bear in mind the following:

Network overhead
> There is some communication overhead to each HTTP request, though it's fairly minimal. After the first client request, the TCP connection remains open until closed by the client.

Per-request transactions
> Each client request is executed in the context of a separate transaction, though there is some support in the REST API for batch operations. For more complex, multistep operations requiring a single transactional context, we should consider using a server extension (see "Server extensions").

Access to Neo4j server is typically by way of its REST API, as discussed previously. The REST API (*http://docs.neo4j.org/chunked/stable/rest-api.html*) comprises JSON-formatted documents over HTTP. Using the REST API we can submit Cypher queries, configure named indexes, and execute several of the built-in graph algorithms. We can also submit JSON-formatted traversal descriptions, and perform batch operations. For the majority of use cases the REST API is sufficient; however, if we need to do something we cannot currently accomplish using the REST API, we should consider developing a server extension.

Server extensions

Server extensions enable us to run Java code inside the server. Using server extensions, we can extend the REST API, or replace it entirely.

Extensions take the form of JAX-RS annotated classes. JAX-RS (*http://jax-rs-spec.java.net/*) is a Java API for building RESTful resources. Using JAX-RS annotations, we decorate each extension class to indicate to the server which HTTP requests it handles. Additional annotations control request and response formats, HTTP headers, and the formatting of URI templates.

Here's an implementation of a simple server extension that allows a client to request the distance between two members of a social network:

```
@Path("/distance")
public class SocialNetworkExtension
{
    private final ExecutionEngine executionEngine;

    public SocialNetworkExtension( @Context GraphDatabaseService db )
    {
        this.executionEngine = new ExecutionEngine( db );
    }
```

```
@GET
@Produces("text/plain")
@Path("/{name1}/{name2}")
public String getDistance  ( @PathParam("name1") String name1,
                             @PathParam("name2") String name2 )
{
    String query = "START first=node:user(name={name1}),\n" +
            "second=node:user(name={name2})\n" +
            "MATCH p=shortestPath(first-[*..4]-second)\n" +
            "RETURN length(p) AS depth";

    Map<String, Object> params = new HashMap<String, Object>();
    params.put( "name1", name1 );
    params.put( "name2", name2 );

    ExecutionResult result = executionEngine.execute( query, params );

    return String.valueOf( result.columnAs( "depth" ).next() );
}
}
```

Of particular interest here are the various annotations:

- @Path("/distance") specifies that this extension will respond to requests directed to relative URIs beginning /distance.

- The @Path("/{name1}/{name2}") annotation on getDistance() further qualifies the URI template associated with this extension. The fragment here is concatenated with /distance to produce /distance/{name1}/{name2}, where {name1} and {name2} are placeholders for any characters occurring between the forward slashes. Later on, in "Testing server extensions" on page 87, we'll register this extension under the /socnet relative URI. At that point, these several different parts of the path ensure that HTTP requests directed to a relative URI beginning /socnet/distance/{name1}/ {name2} (for example, http://<server>/socnet/distance/Ben/Mike) will be dispatched to an instance of this extension.

- @GET specifies that getDistance() should be invoked only if the request is an HTTP GET. @Produces indicates that the response entity body will be formatted as text/ plain.

- The two @PathParam annotations prefacing the parameters to getDistance() serve to map the contents of the {name1} and {name2} path placeholders to the method's name1 and name2 parameters. Given the URI http://<server>/socnet/distance/Ben/ Mike, getDistance() will be invoked with Ben for name1 and Mike for name2.

- The @Context annotation in the constructor causes this extension to be handed a reference to the embedded graph database inside the server. The server infrastructure takes care of creating an extension and injecting it with a graph database instance, but the very presence of the GraphDatabaseService parameter here makes this extension exceedingly testable. As we'll see later, in "Testing server extensions", we can unit test extensions without having to run them inside a server.

Server extensions can be powerful elements in our application architecture. Their chief benefits include:

Complex transactions
> Extensions enable us to execute an arbitrarily complex sequence of operations in the context of a single transaction.

Choice of APIs
> Each extension is injected with a reference to the embedded graph database at the heart of the server. This gives us access to the full range of APIs—Core API, traversal framework, graph algorithm package, and Cypher—for developing our extension's behavior.

Encapsulation
> Because each extension is hidden behind a RESTful interface, we can improve and modify its implementation over time.

Response formats
> We control the response: both the representation format and the HTTP headers. This enables us to create response messages whose contents employ terminology from our domain, rather than the graph-based terminology of the standard REST API (*users*, *products*, and *orders* for example, rather than nodes, relationships, and properties). Further, in controlling the HTTP headers attached to the response, we can leverage the HTTP protocol for things such as caching and conditional requests.

When considering using server extensions, we should bear in mind the following points:

JVM only
> As with developing against embedded Neo4j, we'll have to use a JVM-based language.

GC behaviors
> We can do arbitrarily complex (and dangerous) things inside a server extension. We need to monitor garbage collection behaviors to ensure we don't introduce any untoward side effects.

Clustering

As we discuss in more detail later, in "Availability" on page 157, Neo4j clusters for high availability and horizontal read scaling using master-slave replication. In this section we discuss some of the strategies to consider when using clustered Neo4j.

Replication

Although all writes to a cluster are coordinated through the master, Neo4j does allow writing through slaves, but even then, the slave that's being written to syncs with the master before returning to the client. Because of the additional network traffic and coordination protocol, writing through slaves can be an order of magnitude slower than writing directly to the master. The only reasons for writing through slaves are to increase the durability guarantees of each write (the write is made durable on two instances, rather than one) and to ensure we can read our own writes when employing cache sharding (see "Cache sharding" on page 80 and "Read your own writes" on page 82 later in this chapter). Because newer versions of Neo4j enable us to specify that writes to the master must be replicated out to one or more slaves, thereby increasing the durability guarantees of writes to the master, the case for writing through slaves is now less compelling. Today it is recommended that all writes be directed to the master, and then replicated to slaves using the `ha.tx_push_factor` and `ha.tx_push_strategy` configuration settings (*http://docs.neo4j.org/chunked/milestone/ha-configuration.html*).

Buffer writes using queues

In high write load scenarios, we can use queues to buffer writes and regulate load. With this strategy, writes to the cluster are buffered in a queue; a worker then polls the queue and executes batches of writes against the database. Not only does this regulate write traffic, but it reduces contention, and enables us to pause write operations without refusing client requests during maintenance periods.

Global clusters

For applications catering to a global audience, it is possible to install a multiregion cluster in multiple data centers and on cloud platforms such as Amazon Web Services (AWS). A multiregion cluster enables us to service reads from the portion of the cluster geographically closest to the client. In these situations, however, the latency introduced by the physical separation of the regions can sometimes disrupt the coordination protocol; it is, therefore, often desirable to restrict master reelection to a single region. To achieve this, we create slave-only databases for the instances we don't want to participate in master reelection; we do this by including the `ha.slave_coordinator_up date_mode=none` configuration parameter in an instance's configuration.

Load Balancing

When using a clustered graph database, we should consider load balancing traffic across the cluster to help maximize throughput and reduce latency. Neo4j doesn't include a native load balancer, relying instead on the load-balancing capabilities of the network infrastructure.

Separate read traffic from write traffic

Given the recommendation to direct the majority of write traffic to the master, we should consider clearly separating read requests from write requests. We should configure our load balancer to direct write traffic to the master, while balancing the read traffic across the entire cluster.

In a web-based application, the HTTP method is often sufficient to distinguish a request with a significant side effect—a write—from one that has no significant side effect on the server: POST, PUT, and DELETE can modify server-side resources, whereas GET is side-effect free.

When using server extensions, it's important to distinguish read and write operations using @GET and @POST annotations. If our application depends solely on server extensions, this will suffice to separate the two. If we're using the REST API to submit Cypher queries to the database, however, the situation is not so straightforward. The REST API uses POST as a general "process this" semantic for requests whose contents can include Cypher statements that modify the database. To separate read and write requests in this scenario, we introduce a pair of load balancers: a write load balancer that always directs requests to the master, and a read load balancer that balances requests across the entire cluster. In our application logic, where we know whether the operation is a read or a write, we will then have to decide which of the two addresses we should use for any particular request, as illustrated in Figure 4-9.

When running in server mode, Neo4j exposes a URI that indicates whether that instance is currently the master, and if it isn't, which is. Load balancers can poll this URI at intervals to determine where to route traffic.

Cache sharding

Queries run fastest when the portions of the graph needed to satisfy them reside in main memory (that is, in the filesystem cache and the object cache). A single graph database instance today can hold many billions of nodes, relationships, and properties, meaning that some graphs will be just too big to fit into main memory. Partitioning or sharding a graph is a difficult problem to solve (see "The Holy Grail of Graph Scalability" on page 162). How, then, can we provide for high-performance queries over a very large graph?

One solution is to use a technique called cache sharding (Figure 4-10), which consists of routing each request to a database instance in an HA cluster where the portion of the graph necessary to satisfy that request is *likely* already in main memory (remember: every instance in the cluster will contain a full copy of the data). If the majority of an application's queries are graph-local queries, meaning they start from one or more specific points in the graph, and traverse the surrounding subgraphs, then a mechanism that consistently routes queries beginning from the same set of start points to the same database instance will increase the likelihood of each query hitting a warm cache.

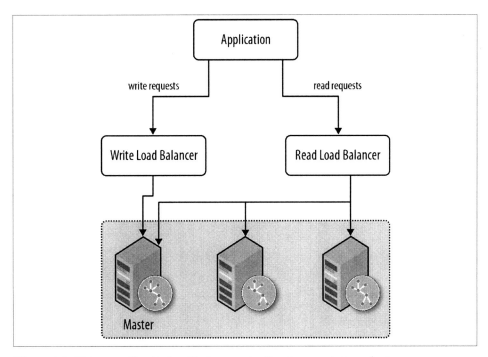

Figure 4-9. Using read/write load balancers to direct requests to a cluster

The strategy used to implement consistent routing will vary by domain. Sometimes it's good enough to have sticky sessions; other times we'll want to route based on the characteristics of the dataset. The simplest strategy is to have the instance that first serves requests for a particular user thereafter serve subsequent requests for that user. Other domain-specific approaches will also work. For example, in a geographical data system we can route requests about particular locations to specific database instances that have been warmed for that location. Both strategies increase the likelihood of the required nodes and relationships already being cached in main memory, where they can be quickly accessed and processed.

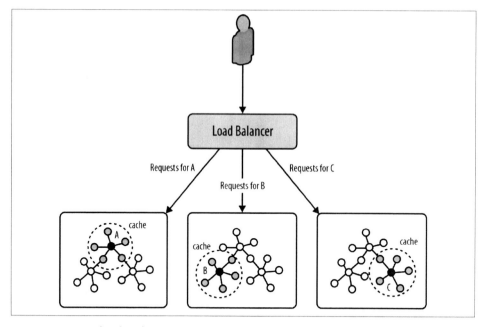

Figure 4-10. Cache sharding

Read your own writes

Occasionally we may need to read our own writes—typically when the application applies an end-user change, and needs on the next request to reflect the effect of this change back to the user. Whereas writes to the master are immediately consistent, the cluster as a whole is eventually consistent. How can we ensure that a write directed to the master is reflected in the next load-balanced read request? One solution is to use the same consistent routing technique used in cache sharding to direct the write to the slave that will be used to service the subsequent read. This assumes that the write and the read can be consistently routed based on some domain criteria in each request.

This is one of the few occasions where it makes sense to write through a slave. But remember: writing through a slave can be an order of magnitude slower than writing directly to the master. We should use this technique sparingly. If a high proportion of our writes require us to read our own write, this technique will significantly impact throughput and latency.

Testing

Testing is a fundamental part of the application development process—not only as a means of verifying that a query or application feature behaves correctly, but also as a way of designing and documenting our application and its data model. Throughout this section we emphasize that testing is an everyday activity; by developing our graph database solution in a test-driven manner, we provide for the rapid evolution of our system, and its continued responsiveness to new business needs.

Test-Driven Data Model Development

In discussing data modeling, we've stressed that our graph model should reflect the kinds of queries we want to run against it. By developing our data model in a test-driven fashion we document our understanding of our domain, and validate that our queries behave correctly.

With test-driven data modeling, we write unit tests based on small, representative example graphs drawn from our domain. These example graphs contain just enough data to communicate a particular feature of the domain; in many cases, they might only comprise 10 or so nodes, plus the relationships that connect them. We use these examples to describe what is normal for the domain, and also what is exceptional. As we discover anomalies and corner cases in our real data, we write a test that reproduces what we've discovered.

The example graphs we create for each test comprise the setup or context for that test. Within this context we exercise a query, and assert that the query behaves as expected. Because we control the context, we, as the author of the test, know what results to expect.

Tests can act like documentation. By reading the tests, developers gain an understanding of the problems and needs the application is intended to address, and the ways in which the authors have gone about addressing them. With this is mind, it's best to use each test to test just one aspect of our domain. It's far easier to read lots of small tests, each of which communicates a discrete feature of our data in a clear, simple, and concise fashion, than it is to reverse engineer a complex domain from a single large and unwieldy test. In many cases, we'll find a particular query being exercised by several tests, some of which demonstrate the happy path through our domain, others of which exercise it in the context of some exceptional structure or set of values.[4]

Over time, we'll build up a suite of tests that can act as a powerful regression test mechanism. As our application evolves, and we add new sources of data, or change the model to meet new needs, our regression test suite will continue to assert that existing features continue to behave as they should. Evolutionary architectures, and the incremental and iterative software development techniques that support them, depend upon a bedrock of asserted behavior. The unit-testing approach to data model development described here enables developers to respond to new business needs with very little risk of undermining or breaking what has come before, confident in the continued quality of the solution.

---

4. Tests not only act as documentation, but they can also be used to generate documentation. All of the Cypher documentation in the Neo4j manual (*http://docs.neo4j.org/chunked/stable/cypher-query-lang.html*) is generated automatically from the unit tests used to develop Cypher.

Example: A test-driven social network data model

In this example we're going to demonstrate developing a very simple Cypher query for a social network. Given the names of a couple of members of the network, our query determines the distance between them.

First we create a small graph that is representative of our domain. Using Cypher, we create a network comprising ten nodes and eight relationships:

```
public GraphDatabaseService createDatabase()
{
    // Create nodes
    String cypher = "CREATE\n" +
            "(ben {name:'Ben'}),\n" +
            "(arnold {name:'Arnold'}),\n" +
            "(charlie {name:'Charlie'}),\n" +
            "(gordon {name:'Gordon'}),\n" +
            "(lucy {name:'Lucy'}),\n" +
            "(emily {name:'Emily'}),\n" +
            "(sarah {name:'Sarah'}),\n" +
            "(kate {name:'Kate'}),\n" +
            "(mike {name:'Mike'}),\n" +
            "(paula {name:'Paula'}),\n" +
            "ben-[:FRIEND]->charlie,\n" +
            "charlie-[:FRIEND]->lucy,\n" +
            "lucy-[:FRIEND]->sarah,\n" +
            "sarah-[:FRIEND]->mike,\n" +
            "arnold-[:FRIEND]->gordon,\n" +
            "gordon-[:FRIEND]->emily,\n" +
            "emily-[:FRIEND]->kate,\n" +
            "kate-[:FRIEND]->paula";

    GraphDatabaseService db =
                new TestGraphDatabaseFactory().newImpermanentDatabase();

    ExecutionEngine engine = new ExecutionEngine( db );
    engine.execute( cypher );

    // Index all nodes in "user" index
    Transaction tx = db.beginTx();
    try
    {
        Iterable<Node> allNodes =
                GlobalGraphOperations.at( db ).getAllNodes();
        for ( Node node : allNodes )
        {
            if ( node.hasProperty( "name" ) )
            {
                db.index().forNodes( "user" )
                        .add( node, "name", node.getProperty( "name" ) );
            }
        }
```

```
        tx.success();
    }
    finally
    {
        tx.finish();
    }

    return db;
}
```

There are two things of interest in createDatabase(). The first is the use of Imperma
nentGraphDatabase, which is a lightweight, in-memory version of Neo4j designed
specifically for unit testing. By using ImpermanentGraphDatabase, we avoid having to
clear up store files on disk after each test. The class can be found in the Neo4j kernel
test jar, which can be obtained with the following dependency reference:

```
<dependency>
    <groupId>org.neo4j</groupId>
    <artifactId>neo4j-kernel</artifactId>
    <version>${project.version}</version>
    <type>test-jar</type>
    <scope>test</scope>
</dependency>
```

ImpermanentGraphDatabase should only be used in unit tests. It is not
a production-ready, in-memory version of Neo4j.

The second thing of interest in createDatabase() is the code for adding nodes to a
named index. Cypher doesn't add the newly created nodes to an index, so for now, we
have to do this manually by iterating all the nodes in the sample graph, adding any with
a name property to the users named index.

Having created a sample graph, we can now write our first test. Here's the test fixture
for testing our social network data model and its queries:

```
public class SocialNetworkTest
{
    private static GraphDatabaseService db;
    private static SocialNetworkQueries queries;

    @BeforeClass
    public static void init()
    {
        db = createDatabase();
        queries = new SocialNetworkQueries( db );
    }

    @AfterClass
    public static void shutdown()
```

```
    {
        db.shutdown();
    }

    @Test
    public void shouldReturnShortestPathBetweenTwoFriends() throws Exception
    {
        // when
        ExecutionResult results = queries.distance( "Ben", "Mike" );

        // then
        assertTrue( results.iterator().hasNext() );
        assertEquals( 4, results.iterator().next().get( "distance" ) );
    }

    // more tests
}
```

This test fixture includes an initialization method, annotated with `@BeforeClass`, which executes before any tests start. Here we call `createDatabase()` to create an instance of the sample graph, and an instance of `SocialNetworkQueries`, which houses the queries under development.

Our first test, `shouldReturnShortestPathBetweenTwoFriends()`, tests that the query under development can find a path between any two members of the network—in this case, `Ben` and `Mike`. Given the contents of the sample graph, we know that `Ben` and `Mike` are connected, but only remotely, at a distance of 4. The test, therefore, asserts that the query returns a nonempty result containing a `distance` value of 4.

Having written the test, we now start developing our first query. Here's the implementation of `SocialNetworkQueries`:

```
public class SocialNetworkQueries
{
    private final ExecutionEngine executionEngine;

    public SocialNetworkQueries( GraphDatabaseService db )
    {
        this.executionEngine = new ExecutionEngine( db );
    }

    public ExecutionResult distance( String firstUser, String secondUser )
    {
        String query = "START first=node:user({firstUserQuery}),\n" +
                "second=node:user({secondUserQuery})\n" +
                "MATCH p=shortestPath(first-[*..4]-second)\n" +
                "RETURN length(p) AS distance";

        Map<String, Object> params = new HashMap<String, Object>();
        params.put( "firstUserQuery", "name:" + firstUser );
        params.put( "secondUserQuery", "name:" + secondUser );
```

```
        return executionEngine.execute( query, params );
    }

    // More queries
}
```

In the constructor for `SocialNetworkQueries` we create a Cypher `ExecutionEngine`, passing in the supplied database instance. We store the execution engine in a member variable, which allows it to be reused over and again throughout the lifetime of the `queries` instance. The query itself we implement in the `distance()` method. Here we create a Cypher statement, initialize a map containing the query parameters, and execute the statement using the execution engine.

If `shouldReturnShortestPathBetweenTwoFriends()` passes (it does), we then go on to test additional scenarios. What happens, for example, if two members of the network are separated by more than four connections? We write up the scenario and what we expect the query to do in another test:

```
@Test
public void shouldReturnNoResultsWhenNoPathUnderAtDistance4OrLess()
    throws Exception
{
    // when
    ExecutionResult results = queries.distance( "Ben", "Arnold" );

    // then
    assertFalse( results.iterator().hasNext() );
}
```

In this instance, this second test passes without us having to modify the underlying Cypher query. In many cases, however, a new test will force us to modify a query's implementation. When that happens, we modify the query to make the new test pass, and then run all the tests in the fixture. A failing test anywhere in the fixture indicates we've broken some existing functionality. We continue to modify the query until all tests are green once again.

Testing server extensions

Server extensions can be developed in a test-driven manner just as easily as embedded Neo4j. Using the simple server extension described earlier, here's how we test it:

```
@Test
public void extensionShouldReturnDistance() throws Exception
{
    // given
    SocialNetworkExtension extension = new SocialNetworkExtension( db );

    // when
    String distance = extension.getDistance( "Ben", "Mike" );
```

```
    // then
    assertEquals( "4", distance );
}
```

Because the extension's constructor accepts a `GraphDatabaseService` instance, we can inject a test instance (an `ImpermanentGraphDatabase` instance), and then call its methods as per any other object.

If, however, we wanted to test the extension running inside a server, we have a little more setup to do:

```
public class SocialNetworkExtensionTest
{
    private static CommunityNeoServer server;

    @BeforeClass
    public static void init() throws IOException
    {
        server = ServerBuilder.server()
                .withThirdPartyJaxRsPackage(
                        "org.neo4j.graphdatabases.queries.server",
                        "/socnet" )
                .build();
        server.start();
        populateDatabase( server.getDatabase().getGraph() );
    }

    @AfterClass
    public static void teardown()
    {
        server.stop();
    }

    @Test
    public void serverShouldReturnDistance() throws Exception
    {
        ClientConfig config = new DefaultClientConfig();
        Client client = Client.create( config );

        WebResource resource = client
                .resource( "http://localhost:7474/socnet/distance/Ben/Mike" );
        ClientResponse response = resource
                .accept( MediaType.TEXT_PLAIN )
                .get( ClientResponse.class );

        assertEquals( 200, response.getStatus() );
        assertEquals( "text/plain",
                response.getHeaders().get( "Content-Type" ).get( 0 ) );
        assertEquals( "4", response.getEntity( String.class ) );
    }
```

```
    // Populate graph
}
```

Here we're using an instance of `CommunityNeoServer` to host the extension. We create the server and populate its database in the test fixture's `init()` method using a `Server Builder`, which is a helper class from Neo4j's server test jar. This builder enables us to register the extension package, and associate it with a relative URI space (in this case, everything below */socnet*). Once `init()` has completed, we have a server instance up and running and listening on port 7474.

In the test itself, `serverShouldReturnDistance()`, we access this server using an HTTP client from the Jersey client library (*http://jersey.java.net/*). The client issues an HTTP GET request for the resource at *http://localhost:7474/socnet/distance/Ben/Mike*. (At the server end, this request is dispatched to an instance of `SocialNetworkExtension`.) When the client receives a response, the test asserts that the HTTP status code, content-type, and content of the response body are correct.

Performance Testing

The test-driven approach that we've described so far communicates context and domain understanding, and tests for correctness. It does not, however, test for performance. What works fast against a small, 20-node sample graph may not work so well when confronted with a much larger graph. Therefore, to accompany our unit tests, we should consider writing a suite of query performance tests. On top of that, we should also invest in some thorough application performance testing early in our application's development life cycle.

Query performance tests

Query performance tests are not the same as full-blown application performance tests. All we're interested in at this stage is whether a particular query performs well when run against a graph that is proportionate to the kind of graph we expect to encounter in production. Ideally, these tests are developed side-by-side with our unit tests. There's nothing worse than investing a lot of time in perfecting a query, only to discover it is not fit for production-sized data.

When creating query performance tests, bear in mind the following guidelines:

- Create a suite of performance tests that exercise the queries developed through our unit testing. Record the performance figures so that we can see the relative effects of tweaking a query, modifying the heap size, or upgrading from one version of a graph database to another.

- Run these tests often, so that we quickly become aware of any deterioration in performance. We might consider incorporating these tests into a continuous delivery build pipeline, failing the build if the test results exceed a certain value.

- Run these tests in-process on a single thread. There's no need to simulate multiple clients at this stage: if the performance is poor for a single client, it's unlikely to improve for multiple clients. Even though they are not, strictly speaking, unit tests, we can drive them using the same unit testing framework we use to develop our unit tests.

- Run each query many times, picking starting nodes at random each time, so that we can see the effect of starting from a cold cache, which is then gradually warmed as multiple queries execute.

Application performance tests

Application performance tests, as distinct from query performance tests, test the performance of the entire application under representative production usage scenarios.

As with query performance tests, we recommend that this kind of performance testing is done as part of everyday development, side-by-side with the development of application features, rather than as a distinct project phase.[5] To facilitate application performance testing early in the project life cycle, it is often necessary to develop a "walking skeleton," an end-to-end slice through the entire system, which can be accessed and exercised by performance test clients. By developing a walking skeleton, we not only provide for performance testing, but we also establish the architectural context for the graph database part of our solution. This enables us to verify our application architecture, and identify layers and abstractions that allow for discrete testing of individual components.

Performance tests serve two purposes: they demonstrate how the system will perform when used in production, and they drive out the operational affordances that make it easier to diagnose performance issues, incorrect behavior, and bugs. What we learn in creating and maintaining a performance test environment will prove invaluable when it comes to deploying and operating the system for real.

When drawing up the criteria for a performance test, we recommend specifying percentiles rather than averages. Never assume a normal distribution of response times: the real world doesn't work like that. For some applications we may want to ensure that *all* requests return within a certain time period. In rare circumstances it may be important for the *very first* request to be as quick as when the caches have been warmed. But in the majority of cases, we will want to ensure the majority of requests return within

---

5. A thorough discussion of agile performance testing can be found in Alistair Jones and Patrick Kua, "Extreme Performance Testing," *The ThoughtWorks Anthology, Volume 2* (Pragmatic Bookshelf, 2012).

a certain time period; that, say, 98% of requests are satisfied in under 200 ms. It is important to keep a record of subsequent test runs so that we can compare performance figures over time, and thereby quickly identify slowdowns and anomalous behavior.

As with unit tests and query performance tests, application performance tests prove most valuable when employed in an automated delivery pipeline, where successive builds of the application are automatically deployed to a testing environment, the tests executed, and the results automatically analyzed. Log files and test results should be stored for later retrieval, analysis, and comparison. Regressions and failures should fail the build, prompting developers to address the issues in a timely manner. One of the big advantages of conducting performance testing over the course of an application's development life cycle, rather than at the end, is that failures and regressions can very often be tied back to a recent piece of development; this enables us to diagnose, pinpoint, and remedy issues rapidly and succinctly.

For generating load, we'll need a load-generating agent. For web applications, there are several open source stress and load testing tools available, including Grinder (*http:// grinder.sourceforge.net/*), JMeter (*http://jmeter.apache.org/*), and Gatling (*http:// gatling-tool.org/*).[6] When testing load-balanced web applications, we should ensure our test clients are distributed across different IP addresses so that requests are balanced across the cluster.

Testing with representative data

For both query performance testing and application performance testing we will need a dataset that is representative of the data we will encounter in production. It will, therefore, be necessary to create or otherwise source such a dataset. In some cases we can obtain a dataset from a third party, or adapt an existing dataset that we own, but unless these datasets are already in the form of a graph, we will have to write some custom export-import code.

In many cases, however, we're starting from scratch. If this is the case, we must dedicate some time to creating a dataset builder. As with the rest of the software development life cycle, this is best done in an iterative and incremental fashion. Whenever we introduce a new element into our domain's data model, as documented and tested in our unit tests, we add the corresponding element to our performance dataset builder. That way, our performance tests will come as close to real-world usage as our current understanding of the domain allows.

When creating a representative dataset, we try to reproduce any domain invariants we have identified: the minimum, maximum, and average number of relationships per node, the spread of different relationship types, property value ranges, and so on. Of

---

6. Max De Marzi describes using Gatling to test Neo4j (*http://bit.ly/101MhGD*).

course, it's not always possible to know these things upfront, and often we'll find ourselves working with rough estimates until such point as production data is available to verify our assumptions.

Although ideally we would always test with a production-sized dataset, it is often not possible or desirable to reproduce extremely large volumes of data in a test environment. In such cases, we should at least ensure that we build a representative dataset whose size exceeds the capacity of the object cache. That way, we'll be able to observe the effect of cache evictions, and querying for portions of the graph not currently held in main memory.

Representative datasets also help with capacity planning. Whether we create a full-sized dataset, or a scaled-down sample of what we expect the production graph to be, our representative dataset will give us some useful figures for estimating the size of the production data on disk. These figures then help us plan how much memory to allocate to the filesystem cache and the Java virtual machine (JVM) heap (see "Capacity Planning" on page 93 for more details).

In the following example we're using a dataset builder called Neode (*https://github.com/iansrobinson/neode*) to build a sample social network:[7]

```
private void createSampleDataset( GraphDatabaseService db )
{
    DatasetManager dsm = new DatasetManager( db, new Log()
    {
        @Override
        public void write( String value )
        {
            System.out.println(value);
        }
    } );

    // User node specification
    NodeSpecification userSpec =
            dsm.nodeSpecification( "user",
                                    indexableProperty( "name" ) );

    // FRIEND relationship specification
    RelationshipSpecification friend =
            dsm.relationshipSpecification( "FRIEND" );

    Dataset dataset =
            dsm.newDataset( "Social network example" );

    // Create user nodes
    NodeCollection users =
```

---

7. Max De Marzi describes an alternative graph generation technique (*http://maxdemarzi.com/2012/07/03/graph-generator/*).

```
                userSpec.create( 1000000 )
                        .update( dataset );


        // Relate users to each other
        users.createRelationshipsTo(
                getExisting( users )
                        .numberOfTargetNodes( minMax( 50, 100 ) )
                        .relationship( friend )
                        .relationshipConstraints( BOTH_DIRECTIONS ) )
                .updateNoReturn( dataset );

        dataset.end();
    }
```

Neode uses node and relationship specifications to describe the nodes and relationships in the graph, together with their properties and permitted property values. Neode then provides a fluent interface for creating and relating nodes.

Capacity Planning

At some point in our application's development life cycle we'll want to start planning for production deployment. In many cases, an organization's project management gating processes mean a project cannot get underway without some understanding of the production needs of the application. Capacity planning is essential both for budgeting purposes and for ensuring there is sufficient lead time for procuring hardware and reserving production resources.

In this section we describe some of the techniques we can use for hardware sizing and capacity planning. Our ability to estimate our production needs depends on a number of factors: the more data we have regarding representative graph sizes, query performance, and the number of expected users and their behaviors, the better our ability to estimate our hardware needs. We can gain much of this information by applying the techniques described in "Testing" on page 82 early in our application development life cycle. In addition, we should understand the cost/performance trade-offs available to us in the context of our business needs.

Optimization Criteria

As we plan our production environment we will be faced with a number of optimization choices. Which we favor will depend upon our business needs:

Cost
> We can optimize for cost by installing the minimum hardware necessary to get the job done.

Performance
> We can optimize for performance by procuring the fastest solution (subject to budgetary constraints).

Redundancy
> We can optimize for redundancy and availability by ensuring the database cluster is big enough to survive a certain number of machine failures (i.e., to survive two machines failing, we will need a cluster comprising five instances).

Load
> With a replicated graph database solution, we can optimize for load by scaling horizontally (for read load), and vertically (for write load).

Performance

Redundancy and load can be costed in terms of the number of machines necessary to ensure availability (five machines to provide continued availability in the face of two machines failing, for example) and scalability (one machine per some number of concurrent requests, as per the calculations in "Load" on page 97). But what about performance? How can we cost performance?

Calculating the cost of graph database performance

In order to understand the cost implications of optimizing for performance, we need to understand the performance characteristics of the database stack. As we describe in more detail later in "Native Graph Storage" on page 144, a graph database uses disk for durable storage, and main memory for caching portions of the graph. In Neo4j, the caching parts of main memory are further divided between the filesystem cache (which is typically managed by the operating system) and the object cache. The filesystem cache is a portion of off-heap RAM into which files on disk are read and cached before being served to the application. The object cache is an on-heap cache that stores object instances of nodes, relationships, and properties.

Spinning disk is by far the slowest part of the database stack. Queries that have to reach all the way down to spinning disk will be orders of magnitude slower than queries that touch only the object cache. Disk access can be improved by using solid-state drives (SSDs) in place of spinning disks, providing an approximate 20 times increase in performance, or by using enterprise flash hardware, which can reduce latencies even further.

Spinning disks and SDDs are cheap, but not very fast. Far more significant performance benefits accrue when the database has to deal only with the caching layers. The filesystem cache offers up to 500 times the performance of spinning disk, whereas the object cache can be up to 5,000 times faster.

For comparative purposes, graph database performance can be expressed as a function of the percentage of data available at each level of the object cache-filesystem cache-disk hierarchy:

(% graph in object cache x 5000) * (% graph in filesystem cache * 500) * 20 (if using SSDs)

An application in which 100% of the graph is available in the object cache (as well as in the filesystem cache, and on disk) will be more performant than one in which 100% is available on disk, but only 80% in the filesystem cache and 20% in the object cache.

Performance optimization options

There are, then, three areas in which we can optimize for performance:

- Increase the object cache (from 2 GB, all the way up to 200 GB or more in exceptional circumstances)
- Increase the percentage of the store mapped into the filesystem cache
- Invest in faster disks: SSDs or enterprise flash hardware

The first two options here require adding more RAM. In costing the allocation of RAM, however, there are a couple of things to bear in mind. First, whereas the size of the store files in the filesystem cache map one-to-one with the size on disk, graph objects in the object cache can be up to 10 times bigger than their on-disk representations. Allocating RAM to the object cache is, therefore, far more expensive per graph element than allocating it to the filesystem cache. The second point to bear in mind relates to the location of the object cache. If our graph database uses an on-heap cache, as does Neo4j, then increasing the size of the cache requires allocating more heap. Most modern JVMs do not cope well with heaps much larger than 8 GB. Once we start growing the heap beyond this size, garbage collection can impact the performance of our application.[8]

As Figure 4-11 shows, the sweet spot for any cost versus performance trade-off lies around the point where we can map our store files in their entirety into RAM, while allowing for a healthy, but modestly sized object cache. Heaps of between 4 and 8 GB are not uncommon, though in many cases, a smaller heap can actually improve performance (by mitigating expensive GC behaviors).

Calculating how much RAM to allocate to the heap and the filesystem cache depends on our knowing the projected size of our graph. Building a representative dataset early in our application's development life cycle will furnish us with some of the data we need to make our calculations. If we cannot fit the entire graph into main memory (that is,

---

8. Neo4j Enterprise Edition includes a cache implementation that mitigates the problems encountered with large heaps, and is being successfully used with heaps in the order of 200 GB.

at a minimum, into the filesystem cache), we should consider cache sharding (see "Cache sharding" on page 80).

 The Neo4j documentation (*http://bit.ly/14p21GZ*) includes details of the size of records and objects that we can use in our calculations. For more general performance and tuning tips, see this site (*http://docs.neo4j.org/chunked/stable/embedded-configuration.html*).

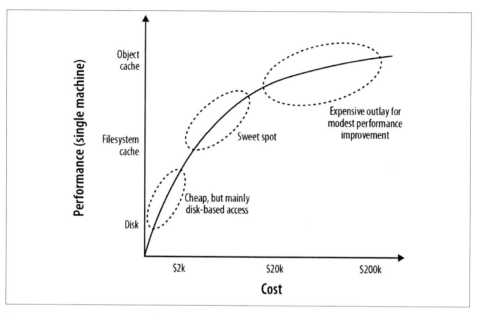

Figure 4-11. Cost versus performance trade-offs

In optimizing a graph database solution for performance, we should bear in mind the following guidelines:

- We should utilize the filesystem cache as much as possible; if possible, we should map our store files in their entirety into this cache

- We should tune the JVM heap and keep an eye on GC behaviors

- We should consider using fast disks—SSDs or enterprise flash hardware—to bring up the bottom line when disk access becomes inevitable

Redundancy

Planning for redundancy requires us to determine how many instances in a cluster we can afford to lose while keeping the application up and running. For non–business-critical applications, this figure might be as low as one (or even zero); once a first instance has failed, another failure will render the application unavailable. Business-critical applications will likely require redundancy of at least two; that is, even after two machines have failed, the application continues serving requests.

For a graph database whose cluster management protocol requires a majority of coordinators to be available to work properly, redundancy of one can be achieved with three or four instances, and redundancy of two with five instances. Four is no better than three in this respect, because if two instances from a four-instance cluster become unavailable, the remaining coordinators will no longer be able to achieve majority.

 Neo4j permits coordinators to be located on separate machines from the database instances in the cluster. This enables us to scale the coordinators independently of the databases. With three database instances and five coordinators located on different machines, we could lose two databases and two coordinators, and still achieve majority, albeit with a lone database.

Load

Optimizing for load is perhaps the trickiest part of capacity planning. As a rule of thumb:

number of concurrent requests = (1000 / average request time (in milliseconds)) * number of cores per machine * number of machines

Actually determining what some of these figures are, or are projected to be, can sometimes be very difficult:

Average request time

This covers the period from when a server receives a request, to when it sends a response. Performance tests can help determine average request time, assuming the tests are running on representative hardware against a representative dataset (we'll have to hedge accordingly if not). In many cases, the "representative dataset" itself is based on a rough estimate; we should modify our figures whenever this estimate changes.

Number of concurrent requests

We should distinguish here between average load and peak load. Determining the number of concurrent requests a new application must support is a difficult thing to do. If we're replacing or upgrading an existing application, we may have access to some recent production statistics we can use to refine our estimates. Some organizations are able to extrapolate from existing application data the likely requirements for a new application. Other than that, it's down to our stakeholders to estimate the projected load on the system, but we must beware of inflated expectations.

Summary

In this chapter we've discussed the most important aspects of developing a graph database application. We've seen how to create graph models that address an application's needs and an end user's goals, and how to make those models and associated queries expressive and robust using unit and performance tests. We've looked at the pros and cons of a couple of different application architectures, and enumerated the factors we need to consider when planning for production.

In the next chapter we'll look at how graph databases are being used today to solve real-world problems in domains as varied as social networking, recommendations, master data management, data center management, access control, and logistics.

CHAPTER 5

Graphs in the Real World

In this chapter we look at some of the common real-world use cases for graph databases and identify the reasons why organizations choose to use a graph database rather than a relational or other NOSQL store. The bulk of the chapter comprises three in-depth use cases, with details of the relevant data models and queries. Each of these examples has been drawn from a real-world production system; the names, however, have been changed, and the technical details simplified where necessary to hide any accidental complexity, and thereby highlight key design points.

Why Organizations Choose Graph Databases

Throughout this book, we've sung the praises of the graph data model, its power and flexibility, and its innate expressiveness. When it comes to applying a graph database to a real-world problem, with real-world technical and business constraints, organizations choose graph databases for the following reasons:

"Minutes to milliseconds" performance
> Query performance and responsiveness are top of many organizations' concerns with regard to their data platforms. Online transactional systems, large web applications in particular, must respond to end users in milliseconds if they are to be successful. In the relational world, as an application's dataset size grows, join pains begin to manifest themselves, and performance deteriorates. Using index-free adjacency, a graph database turns complex joins into fast graph traversals, thereby maintaining millisecond performance irrespective of the overall size of the dataset.

Drastically accelerated development cycles
> The graph data model reduces the impedance mismatch that has plagued software development for decades, thereby reducing the development overhead of translating back and forth between an object model and a tabular relational model. More importantly, the graph model reduces the impedance mismatch between the

technical and business domains: subject matter experts, architects, and developers can talk about and picture the core domain using a shared model that is then incorporated into the application itself.

Extreme business responsiveness

Successful applications rarely stay still; changes in business conditions, user behaviors, and technical and operational infrastructures drive new requirements. In the past, this has required organizations to undertake careful and lengthy data migrations that involve modifying schemas, transforming data, and maintaining redundant data to serve old and new features. The schema-free nature of a graph database coupled with the ability to simultaneously relate data elements in lots of different ways allows a graph database solution to evolve as the business evolves, reducing risk and time-to-market.

Enterprise ready

Data is important: when employed in a business-critical application, a data technology must be robust, scalable, and more often than not, transactional. Although some graph databases are fairly new and not yet fully mature, there are graph databases on the market that provide all the *-ilities*—ACID (Atomic, Consistent, Isolated, Durable) transactionality, high-availability, horizontal read scalability, and storage of billions of entities—needed by large enterprises today, as well as the performance and flexibility characteristics discussed previously. This has been an important factor leading to the adoption of graph databases by organizations: not merely in modest offline or departmental capacities, but in ways that can truly change the business.

Common Use Cases

In this section we describe some of the most common graph database use cases, identifying how the graph model and the specific characteristics of the graph database can be applied to generate competitive insight and significant business value.

Social

We are only just beginning to discover the power of social data. In their book *Connected*, social scientists Nicholas Christakis and James Fowler show how, despite knowing nothing about an individual, we can better predict that person's behavior by understanding who he is connected to, than we can by accumulating facts about him.[1]

Social applications allow organizations to gain competitive and operational advantage by leveraging information about the connections between people, together with discrete

---

1. See Nicholas Christakis and James Fowler, *Connected: The Amazing Power of Social Networks and How They Shape Our Lives* (HarperPress, 2011).

information about individuals, to facilitate collaboration and flow of information, and predict behavior.

As Facebook's use of the term *social graph* implies, graph data models and graph databases are a natural fit for this overtly relationship-centered domain. Social networks help us identify the direct *and* indirect relationships between people, groups, and the things with which they interact, allowing users to rate, review, and discover each other and the things they care about. By understanding who interacts with whom, how people are connected, and what representatives within a group are likely to do or choose based on the aggregate behavior of the group, we generate tremendous insight into the unseen forces that influence individual behaviors. We discuss predictive modeling and its role in social network analysis in more detail in "Graph Theory and Predictive Modeling" on page 174.

Social relations may be either explicit or implicit. Explicit relations occur wherever social subjects volunteer a direct link—by liking someone on Facebook, for example, or indicating someone is a current or former colleague, as happens on LinkedIn. Implicit relations emerge out of other relationships that indirectly connect two or more subjects by way of an intermediary. We can relate subjects based on their opinions, likes, purchases, and even the products of their day-to-day work. Such indirect relationships lend themselves to being applied in multiple suggestive and inferential ways: we can say that A is *likely* to know, or like, or otherwise connect to B based on some common intermediaries. In so doing, we move from social network analysis into the realm of recommendation engines.

Recommendations

Effective recommendations are a prime example of generating end-user value through the application of an inferential or suggestive capability. Whereas line-of-business applications typically apply deductive and precise algorithms—calculating payroll, applying tax, and so on—to generate end-user value, recommendation algorithms are inductive and suggestive, identifying people, products, or services an individual or group is *likely* to have some interest in.

Recommendation algorithms establish relationships between people and things: other people, products, services, media content—whatever is relevant to the domain in which the recommendation is employed. Relationships are established based on users' behaviors, whether purchasing, producing, consuming, rating, or reviewing the resources in question. The engine can then identify resources of interest to a particular individual or group, or individuals and groups likely to have some interest in a particular resource. With the first approach, identifying resources of interest to a specific user, the behavior of the user in question—her purchasing behavior, expressed preferences, and attitudes as expressed in ratings and reviews—are correlated with those of other users in order to identify similar users and thereafter the things with which they are connected. The second approach, identifying users and groups for a particular resource, focuses on the characteristics of the resource in question; the engine then identifies similar resources, and the users associated with those resources.

As in the social use case, making an effective recommendation depends on understanding the connections between things, as well as the quality and strength of those connections—all of which are best expressed as a property graph. Queries are primarily graph local, in that they start with one or more identifiable subjects, whether people or resources, and thereafter discover surrounding portions of the graph.

Taken together, social networks and recommendation engines provide key differentiating capabilities in the areas of retail, recruitment, sentiment analysis, search, and knowledge management. Graphs are a good fit for the densely connected data structures germane to each of these areas; storing and querying this data using a graph database allows an application to surface end-user real-time results that reflect recent changes to the data, rather than precalculated, stale results.

Geo

Geospatial is the original graph use case: Euler solved the Seven Bridges of Königsberg problem by positing a mathematical theorem that later came to form the basis of graph theory. Geospatial applications of graph databases range from calculating routes between locations in an abstract network such as a road or rail network, airspace network, or logistical network (as illustrated by the logistics example later in this chapter) to spatial operations such as find all points of interest in a bounded area, find the center of a region, and calculate the intersection between two or more regions.

Geospatial operations depend upon specific data structures, ranging from simple weighted and directed relationships, through to spatial indexes, such as R-Trees (*http:// en.wikipedia.org/wiki/R-tree*), which represent multidimensional properties using tree data structures. As indexes, these data structures naturally take the form of a graph, typically hierarchical in form, and as such they are a good fit for a graph database. Because of the schema-free nature of graph databases, geospatial data can reside in the database beside other kinds of data—social network data, for example—allowing for complex multidimensional querying across several domains.[2]

Geospatial applications of graph databases are particularly relevant in the areas of telecommunications, logistics, travel, timetabling, and route planning.

---

2. Neo4j Spatial (*https://github.com/neo4j/spatial*) is an open source library of utilities that implement spatial indexes and expose Neo4j data to geotools.

Master Data Management

Master data is data that is critical to the operation of a business, but which itself is non-transactional. Master data includes data concerning users, customers, products, suppliers, departments, geographies, sites, cost centers, and business units. In large organizations, this data is often held in many different places, with lots of overlap and redundancy, in many different formats, and with varying degrees of quality and means of access. *Master Data Management* (MDM) is the practice of identifying, cleaning, storing, and, most importantly, governing this data. Its key concerns include managing change over time as organizational structures change, businesses merge, and business rules change; incorporating new sources of data; supplementing existing data with externally sourced data; addressing the needs of reporting, compliance, and business intelligence consumers; and versioning data as its values and schemas change.

Graph databases don't provide a full MDM solution; they are, however, ideally applied to the modeling, storing, and querying of hierarchies, master data metadata, and master data models. Such models include type definitions, constraints, relationships between entities, and the mappings between the model and the underlying source systems. A graph database's structured yet schema-free data model provides for ad hoc, variable, and exceptional structures—schema anomalies that commonly arise when there are multiple redundant data sources—while at the same time allowing for the rapid evolution of the master data model in line with changing business needs.

Network and Data Center Management

In Chapter 3 we looked at a simple data center domain model, showing how the physical and virtual assets inside a data center can be easily modeled with a graph. Communications networks are graph structures; graph databases are, therefore, a great fit for modeling, storing, and querying this kind of domain data. The distinction between network management of a large communications network versus data center management is largely a matter of which side of the firewall you're working. For all intents and purposes, these two things are one and the same.

A graph representation of a network enables us to catalogue assets, visualize how they are deployed, and identify the dependencies between them. The graph's connected structure, together with a query language like Cypher, enable us to conduct sophisticated impact analyses, answering questions such as:

- Which parts of the network—which applications, services, virtual machines, physical machines, data centers, routers, switches, and fibre—do important customers depend on? (Top-down analysis)
- Conversely, which applications and services, and ultimately, customers, in the network will be affected if a particular network element—a router or switch, for example—fails? (Bottom-up analysis)

- Is there redundancy throughout the network for the most important customers?

Graph database solutions complement existing network management and analysis tools. As with master data management, they can be used to bring together data from disparate inventory systems, providing a single view of the network and its consumers, from the smallest network element all the way to application and services and the customers who use them. A graph database representation of the network can also be used to enrich operational intelligence based on event correlations: whenever an event correlation engine [a Complex Event Processor (*http://en.wikipedia.org/wiki/Complex_event_processing*), for example] infers a complex event from a stream of low-level network events, it can assess the impact of that event using the graph model, and thereafter trigger any necessary compensating or mitigating actions.

Today, graph databases are being successfully employed in the areas of telecommunications, network management and analysis, cloud platform management, data center and IT asset management, and network impact analysis, where they are reducing impact analysis and problem resolution times from days and hours down to minutes and seconds. Performance, flexibility in the face of changing network schemas, and fit for the domain are all important factors here.

Authorization and Access Control (Communications)

Authorization and access control solutions store information about parties (e.g., administrators, organizational units, end-users) and resources (e.g., files, shares, network devices, products, services, agreements), together with the rules governing access to those resources; they then apply these rules to determine who can access or manipulate a resource. Access control has traditionally been implemented either using directory services or by building a custom solution inside an application's backend. Hierarchical directory structures, however, cannot cope with the nonhierarchical organizational and resource dependency structures that characterize multiparty distributed supply chains. Hand-rolled solutions, particularly those developed on a relational database, suffer join pain as the dataset size grows, becoming slow and unresponsive, and ultimately delivering a poor end-user experience.

A graph database can store complex, densely connected access control structures spanning billions of parties and resources. Its structured yet schema-free data model supports both hierarchical and nonhierarchical structures, while its extensible property model allows for capturing rich metadata regarding every element in the system. With a query engine that can traverse millions of relationships per second, access lookups over large, complex structures execute in milliseconds.

As with network management and analysis, a graph database access control solution allows for both top-down and bottom-up queries:

- Which resources—company structures, products, services, agreements, and end users—can a particular administrator manage? (Top-down)

- Which resource can an end user access?

- Given a particular resource, who can modify its access settings? (Bottom-up)

Graph database access control and authorization solutions are particularly applicable in the areas of content management, federated authorization services, social networking preferences, and software as a service (SaaS) offerings, where they realize minutes to milliseconds increases in performance over their hand-rolled, relational predecessors.

Real-World Examples

In this section we describe three example use cases in detail: social and recommendations, authorization and access control, and logistics. Each use case is drawn from one or more production applications of a graph database (specifically in these cases, Neo4j). Company names, context, data models, and queries have been tweaked to eliminate accidental complexity and to highlight important design and implementation choices.

Social Recommendations (Professional Social Network)

Talent.net is a social recommendations application that enables users to discover their own professional network, and identify other users with particular skill sets. Users work for companies, work on projects, and have one or more interests or skills. Based on this information, Talent.net can describe a user's professional network by identifying other subscribers who share his or her interests. Searches can be restricted to the user's current company, or extended to encompass the entire subscriber base. Talent.net can also identify individuals with specific skills who are directly or indirectly connected to the current user; such searches are useful when looking for a subject matter expert for a current engagement.

Talent.net illustrates how a powerful inferential capability can be developed using a graph database. Although many line-of-business applications are deductive and precise —calculating tax or salary, or balancing debits and credits, for example—a new seam of end-user value opens up when we apply inductive algorithms to our data. This is what Talent.net does. Based on people's interests and skills, and their work history, the application can suggest likely candidates for including in one's professional network. These results are not precise in the way a payroll calculation must be precise, but they are extremely useful nonetheless.

Talent.net infers connections between people. Contrast this with LinkedIn, for example, where users explicitly declare they know or have worked with someone. This is not to say that LinkedIn is solely a precise social networking capability, because it too applies inductive algorithms to generate further insight. But with Talent.net even the primary tie, (A)-[:KNOWS]->(B), is inferred, rather than volunteered.

Today, Talent.net depends on users having supplied information regarding their interests, skills, and work history before it can infer their professional social relations. But with the core inferential capabilities in place, the platform is set to generate even greater insight for less end-user effort. Skills and interests, for example, can be inferred from the processes and products surrounding people's day-to-day work activities. Writing code, writing documents, exchanging emails: activities such as these require interacting with systems that allow us to capture hints as to a person's skills. Other sources of data that help contextualize a user include group memberships and meetup lists. Although the use case presented here does not cover these higher-order inferential features, their implementation requires mostly application integration and partnership agreements rather than any significant change to the graph or the algorithms used.

Talent.net data model

To help describe the Talent.net data model, we've created a small sample graph, as shown in Figure 5-1, which we'll use throughout this section to illustrate the Cypher queries behind the main Talent.net use cases.

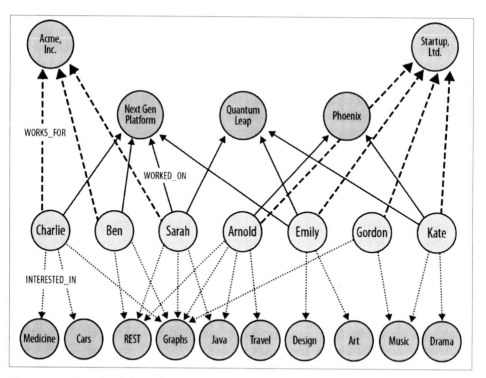

Figure 5-1. Sample of the Talent.net social network

The sample graph shown here has just two companies, each with several employees. An employee is connected to his employer by a WORKS_FOR relationship. Each employee is INTERESTED_IN one or more topics, and has WORKED_ON one or more projects. Occasionally, employees from different companies work on the same project.

This structure addresses two important use cases:

- Given a user, inferring social relations—that is, identifying their professional social network—based on shared interests and skills.
- Given a user, recommend someone that they have worked with, or who has worked with people they have worked with, who has a particular skill.

The first use case helps build communities around shared interests; the second helps identify people to fill specific project roles.

Inferring social relations

Talent.net's graph allows it to infer a user's professional social network by following the relationships that connect an individual's interests to other people. The strength of the recommendation depends on the number of shared interests. If Sarah is interested in Java, graphs, and REST, Ben in graphs and REST, and Charlie in graphs, cars, and medicine, then there is a likely tie between Sarah and Ben based on their mutual interest in graphs and REST, and another tie between Sarah and Charlie based on their mutual interest in graphs, with the tie between Sarah and Ben stronger than the one between Sarah and Charlie (two shared interests versus one).

Figure 5-2 shows the pattern representing colleagues who share a user's interests. The subject node refers to the subject of the query (in the preceding example, this is Sarah). This node can be looked up in an index. The remaining nodes will be discovered once the pattern is anchored to the subject node and then flexed around the graph.

The Cypher to implement this query is shown here:

```
START  subject=node:user(name={name})
MATCH  (subject)-[:WORKS_FOR]->(company)<-[:WORKS_FOR]-(person),
       (subject)-[:INTERESTED_IN]->(interest)<-[:INTERESTED_IN]-(person)
RETURN person.name AS name,
       count(interest) AS score,
       collect(interest.name) AS interests
ORDER BY score DESC
```

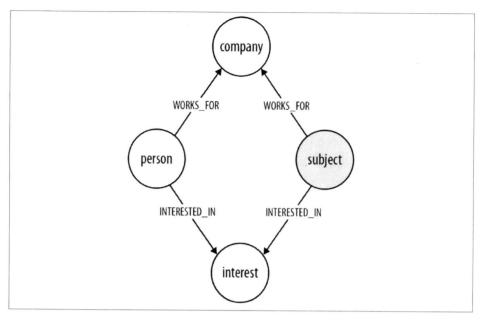

Figure 5-2. Pattern to find colleagues who share a user's interests

The query works as follows:

- START looks up the subject of the query in the user index, and assigns the result to the subject identifier.

- MATCH then matches this person with people who work for the same company, and who share one or more of their interests. If the subject of the query is Sarah, who works for Acme, then in the case of Ben, MATCH will match twice: ('Acme')<-[:WORKS_FOR]-('Ben')-[:INTERESTED_IN]->('graphs') and ('Acme')<-[:WORKS_FOR]-('Ben')-[:INTERESTED_IN]->('REST'). In the case of Charlie, it will match once: ('Acme')<-[:WORKS_FOR]-('Charlie')-[:INTERESTED_IN]->('graphs').

- RETURN creates a projection of the matched data: for each matched colleague, we extract their name, count the number of interests they have in common with the subject of the query (aliasing this result as score), and, using collect, create a comma-separated list of these mutual interests. Where a person has multiple matches, as does Ben in our example, count and collect aggregate their matches into a single row in the returned results (in fact, both count and collect can perform this aggregating function independently of one another).

- Finally, we order the results based on each colleague's score, highest first.

Running this query against our sample graph, with Sarah as the subject, yields the following results:

```
+----------------------------------------+
| name       | score | interests         |
+----------------------------------------+
| "Ben"      | 2     | ["Graphs","REST"] |
| "Charlie"  | 1     | ["Graphs"]        |
+----------------------------------------+
2 rows
```

Figure 5-3 shows the portion of the graph that was matched to generate these results.

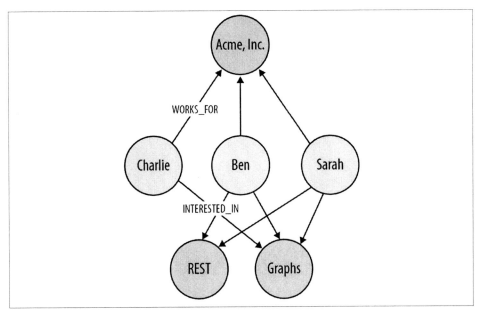

Figure 5-3. Colleagues who share Sarah's interests

Notice that this query only finds people who work for the same company as Sarah. If we want to extend the search to find people who work for other companies, we need to modify the query slightly:

```
START   subject=node:user(name={name})
MATCH   (subject)-[:INTERESTED_IN]->(interest)<-[:INTERESTED_IN]-(person),
        (person)-[:WORKS_FOR]->(company)
RETURN  person.name AS name,
        company.name AS company,
        count(interest) AS score,
        collect(interest.name) AS interests
ORDER BY score DESC
```

The changes are as follows:

- In the MATCH clause, we no longer require matched persons to work for the same company as the subject of the query. (We do, however, still capture the company for whom each matched person works, because we want to return this information in the results.)

- In the RETURN clause we now include the company details for each matched person.

Running this query against our sample data returns the following results:

```
+-----------------------------------------------------------------+
| name      | company        | score | interests                 |
+-----------------------------------------------------------------+
| "Arnold"  | "Startup, Ltd" | 3     | ["Java","Graphs","REST"]  |
| "Ben"     | "Acme, Inc"    | 2     | ["Graphs","REST"]         |
| "Gordon"  | "Startup, Ltd" | 1     | ["Graphs"]                |
| "Charlie" | "Acme, Inc"    | 1     | ["Graphs"]                |
+-----------------------------------------------------------------+
4 rows
```

Figure 5-4 shows the portion of the graph that was matched to generate these results.

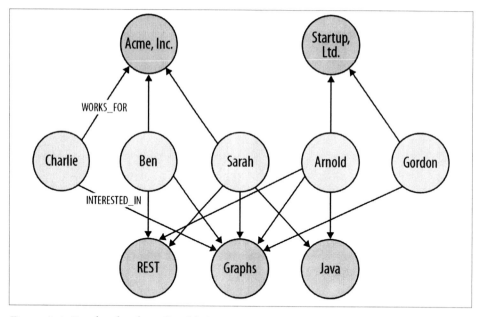

Figure 5-4. People who share Sarah's interests

Although Ben and Charlie still figure in the results, it turns out that Arnold, who works for Startup, Ltd., has most in common with Sarah: three topics compared to Ben's two and Charlie's one.

Finding colleagues with particular interests

In the second Talent.net use case, we turn from inferring social relations based on shared interests to finding individuals who have a particular skillset, and who have either worked with the person who is the subject of the query, or worked with people who have worked with the subject. By applying the graph in this manner, we can find individuals to staff project roles based on their social ties to people we trust—or at least have worked with.

The social ties in question arise from individuals having worked on the same project. Contrast this with the previous use case, where the social ties were inferred based on shared interests. If people have worked on the same project, we infer a social tie. The projects, then, form intermediate nodes that bind two or more people together: they are instances of collaboration that have brought people into contact with one another. Anyone we discover in this fashion is a candidate for including in our results—as long as they possess the interests or skills we are looking for.

Here's a Cypher query that finds colleagues, and colleagues-of-colleagues, who have one or more particular interests:

```
START subject=node:user(name={name})
MATCH p=(subject)-[:WORKED_ON]->()-[:WORKED_ON*0..2]-()
        <-[:WORKED_ON]-(person)-[:INTERESTED_IN]->(interest)
WHERE person<>subject AND interest.name IN {interests}
WITH person, interest, min(length(p)) as pathLength
RETURN person.name AS name,
       count(interest) AS score,
       collect(interest.name) AS interests,
       ((pathLength - 1)/2) AS distance
ORDER BY score DESC
LIMIT {resultLimit}
```

This is quite a complex query. Let's break it down little, and look at each part in more detail:

- START looks up the subject of the query in the user index, and assigns the result to the subject identifier.

- MATCH finds people who are connected to the subject by way of having worked on the same project, or having worked on the same project as people who have worked with the subject. For each person we match, we capture his interests. This match is then further refined by the WHERE clause, which excludes nodes that match the subject of the query, and ensures we only match people who are interested in the things we care about. For each successful match, we assign the entire path of the match—that is, the path that extends from the subject of the query all the way through the matched person to his interest—to the identifier p. We'll look at this MATCH clause in more detail shortly.

- WITH pipes the results to the RETURN clause, filtering out redundant paths as it does so. Redundant paths are present in the results at this point because colleagues and colleagues-of-colleagues are often reachable through different paths, some longer than others. We want to filter these longer paths out. That's exactly what the WITH clause does. The WITH clause emits triples comprising a person, an interest, and the length of the path from the subject of the query through the person to his interest. Given that any particular person/interest combination may appear more than once in the results, but with different path lengths, we want to aggregate these multiple lines by collapsing them to a triple containing only the shortest path, which we do using min(length(p)) as pathLength.

- RETURN creates a projection of the data, performing more aggregation as it does so. The data piped by the WITH clause to RETURN contains one entry per person per interest: if a person matches two of the supplied interests, there will be two separate data entries. We aggregate these entries using count and collect: count to create an overall score for a person, collect to create a comma-separated list of matched interests for that person. As part of the results, we also calculate how far the matched person is from the subject of the query: we take the pathLength for that person, subtract one (for the INTERESTED_IN relationship at the end of the path), and then divide by two (because the person is separated from the subject by pairs of WORKED_ON relationships). Finally, we order the results based on score, highest score first, and limit them according to a resultLimit parameter supplied by the query's client.

The MATCH clause in the preceding query uses a variable-length path, [:WORKED_ON*0..2], as part of a larger pattern to match people who have worked directly with the subject of the query, as well as people who have worked on the same project as people who have worked with the subject. Because each person is separated from the subject of the query by one or two pairs of WORKED_ON relationships, Talent.net could have written this portion of the query as MATCH p=(subject)-[:WORKED_ON*2..4]-(person)-[:INTERESTED_IN]->(interest), with a variable-length path of between two and four WORKED_ON relationships. However, long variable-length paths can be relatively inefficient. When writing such queries, it is advisable to restrict variable-length paths to as narrow a scope as possible. To increase the performance of the query, Talent.net uses a fixed-length outgoing WORKED_ON relationship that extends from the subject to her first project, and another fixed-length WORKED_ON relationship that connects the matched person to a project, with a smaller variable-length path in between.

Running this query against our sample graph, and again taking Sarah as the subject of the query, if we look for colleagues and colleagues-of-colleagues who have interests in Java, travel, or medicine, we get the following results:

```
+-------------------------------------------------------+
| name      | score | interests           | distance |
+-------------------------------------------------------+
| "Arnold"  | 2     | ["Travel","Java"]   | 2        |
| "Charlie" | 1     | ["Medicine"]        | 1        |
+-------------------------------------------------------+
2 rows
```

Note that the results are ordered by `score`, not `distance`. Arnold has two out of the three interests, and therefore scores higher than Charlie, who only has one, even though he is at two removes from Sarah, whereas Charlie has worked directly with Sarah.

Figure 5-5 shows the portion of the graph that was traversed and matched to generate these results.

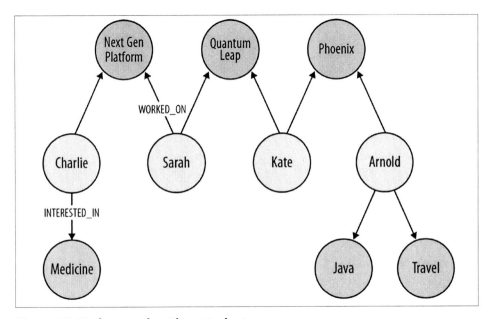

Figure 5-5. Finding people with particular interests

Let's take a moment to understand how this query executes in more detail. Figure 5-6 shows three stages in the execution of the query. The first stage shows each of the paths as they are matched by the `MATCH` and `WHERE` clauses. As we can see, there is one redundant path: `Charlie` is matched directly, through `Next Gen Platform`, but also indirectly, by way of `Quantum Leap` and `Emily`. The second stage represents the filtering that takes place in the `WITH` clause. Here we emit triples comprising the matched person, the matched interest, and the length of the shortest path from the subject through the matched person to her interest. The third stage represents the `RETURN` clause, wherein we aggregate the results on behalf of each matched person, and calculate her score and distance from the subject.

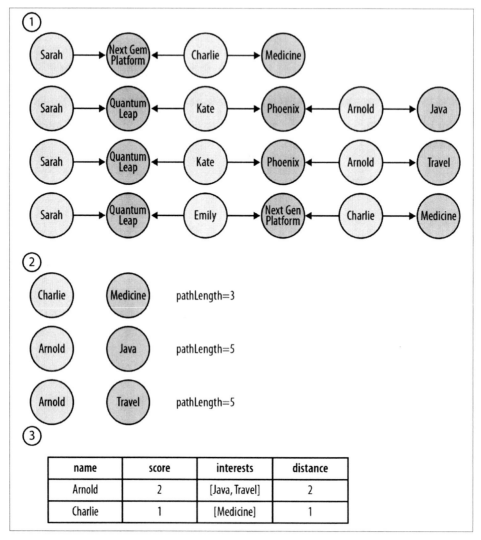

Figure 5-6. Query pipeline

Adding WORKED_WITH relationships

The query for finding colleagues and colleagues-of-colleagues with particular interests is the one most frequently executed on Talent.net's site, and the success of the site depends in large part on its performance. The query uses pairs of WORKED_ON relationships (for example, ('Sarah')-[:WORKED_ON]->('Next Gen Platform')<-[:WORKED_ON]-('Charlie')) to infer that users have worked with one another. Although reasonably performant, this is nonetheless inefficient, because it requires traversing two explicit relationships to infer the presence of a single implicit relationship.

To eliminate this inefficiency, Talent.net now precomputes WORKED_WITH relationships, thereby enriching the data and providing shorter paths for these performance-critical access patterns. As we discussed in "Iterative and Incremental Development" on page 72, it's quite common to optimize graph access by adding a direct relationship between two nodes that would otherwise be connected only by way of intermediaries.

In terms of the Talent.net domain, WORKED_WITH is a bidirectional relationship. In the graph, however, it is implemented using a unidirectional relationship. Although a relationship's direction can often add useful semantics to its definition, in this instance the direction is meaningless. This isn't a significant issue, so long as queries that operate with WORKED_WITH relationships ignore the relationship direction.

Calculating a user's WORKED_WITH relationships and adding them to the graph isn't difficult, nor is it particularly expensive in terms of resource consumption. It can, however, add milliseconds to any end-user interactions that update a user's profile with new project information, so Talent.net has decided to perform this operation asynchronously to end-user activities. Whenever a user changes his project history, Talent.net adds a job that recalculates that user's WORKED_WITH relationships to a queue. A single writer thread polls this queue and executes the jobs using the following Cypher statement:

```
START subject = node:user(name={name})
MATCH (subject)-[:WORKED_ON]->()<-[:WORKED_ON]-(person)
WHERE NOT((subject)-[:WORKED_WITH]-(person))
WITH DISTINCT subject, person
CREATE UNIQUE (subject)-[:WORKED_WITH]-(person)
RETURN subject.name AS startName, person.name AS endName
```

Figure 5-7 shows what our sample graph looks like once it has been enriched with WORKED_WITH relationships.

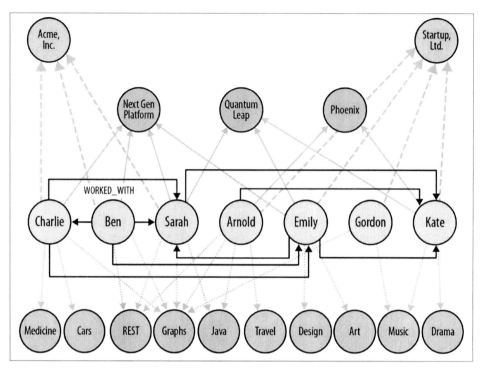

Figure 5-7. Talent.net graph enriched with WORKED_WITH relationships

Using the enriched graph, Talent.net now finds colleagues and colleagues-of-colleagues with particular interests using a slightly simpler version of the query we looked at earlier:

```
START subject=node:user(name={name})
MATCH p=(subject)-[:WORKED_WITH*0..1]-()-[:WORKED_WITH]-(person)
        -[:INTERESTED_IN]->(interest)
WHERE person<>subject AND interest.name IN {interests}
WITH person, interest, min(length(p)) as pathLength
RETURN person.name AS name,
        count(interest) AS score,
        collect(interest.name) AS interests,
        (pathLength - 1) AS distance
ORDER BY score DESC
LIMIT {resultLimit}
```

Authorization and Access Control

TeleGraph Communications is an international communications services company. Millions of domestic and business users subscribe to its products and services. For several years, it has offered its largest business customers the ability to self-service their accounts. Using a browser-based application, administrators within each of these customer organizations can add and remove services on behalf of their employees. To ensure that users and administrators see and change only those parts of the organization and the products and services they are entitled to manage, the application employs a complex access control system, which assigns privileges to many millions of users across tens of millions of product and service instances.

TeleGraph has decided to replace the existing access control system with a graph database solution. There are two drivers here: performance and business responsiveness.

Performance issues have dogged TeleGraph's self-service application for several years. The original system is based on a relational database, which uses recursive joins to model complex organizational structures and product hierarchies, and stored procedures to implement the access control business logic. Because of the join-intensive nature of the data model, many of the most important queries are unacceptably slow: for large companies, generating a view of the things an administrator can manage takes many minutes. This creates a very poor user experience, and hampers the revenue-generating capabilities of the self-service offering.

The performance issues that affect the original application suggest it is no longer fit for today's needs, never mind tomorrow's. TeleGraph has ambitious plans to move into new regions and markets, effectively increasing its customer base by an order of magnitude. The existing solution clearly cannot accommodate the needs of this new strategy. A graph database solution, in contrast, offers the performance, scalability, and adaptiveness necessary for dealing with a rapidly changing market.

TeleGraph data model

Figure 5-8 shows a sample of the TeleGraph data model.

This model comprises two hierarchies. In the first hierarchy, administrators within each customer organization are assigned to groups; these groups are then accorded various permissions against that organization's organizational structure:

- `ALLOWED_INHERIT` connects an administrator group to an organizational unit, thereby allowing administrators within that group to manage the organizational unit. This permission is inherited by children of the parent organizational unit. We see an example of inherited permissions in the TeleGraph example data model in the relationships between `Group 1` and `Acme`, and the child of `Acme`, `Spinoff`. `Group 1` is connected to `Acme` using an `ALLOWED_INHERIT` relationship. `Ben`, as a member of `Group 1`, can manage employees both of `Acme` *and* `Spinoff` thanks to this `AL LOWED_INHERIT` relationship.

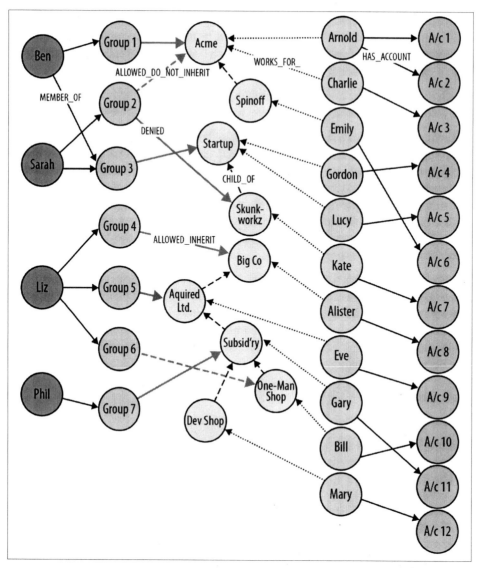

Figure 5-8. Access control graph

- ALLOWED_DO_NOT_INHERIT connects an administrator group to an organizational unit in a way that allows administrators within that group to manage the organizational unit, but not any of its children. Sarah, as a member of Group 2, can administer Acme, but not its child Spinoff, because Group 2 is connected to Acme by an ALLOWED_DO_NOT_INHERIT relationship, not an ALLOWED_INHERIT relationship.

- DENIED forbids administrators from accessing an organizational unit. This permission is inherited by children of the parent organizational unit. In the TeleGraph diagram, this is best illustrated by Liz and her permissions with respect to Big Co, Acquired Ltd, Subsidiary, and One-Map Shop. As a result of her membership of Group 4 and its ALLOWED_INHERIT permission on Big Co, Liz can manage Big Co. But despite this being an inheritable relationship, Liz cannot manage Acquired Ltd or Subsidiary; the reason being, Group 5, of which Liz is a member, is DENIED access to Acquired Ltd and its children (which includes Subsidiary). Liz can, however, manage One-Map Shop, thanks to an ALLOWED_DO_NOT_INHERIT permission granted to Group 6, the last group to which Liz belongs.

DENIED takes precedence over ALLOWED_INHERIT, but is subordinate to ALLOWED_DO_NOT_INHERIT. Therefore, if an administrator is connected to a company by way of ALLOWED_DO_NOT_INHERIT and DENIED, ALLOWED_DO_NOT_INHERIT prevails.

Fine-Grained Relationships, or Relationships with Properties?

Notice that the TeleGraph access control data model uses fine-grained relationships (ALLOWED_INHERIT, ALLOWED_DO_NOT_INHERIT, and DENIED) rather than a single relationship type qualified by properties—something like PERMISSION with allowed and inherited boolean properties. TeleGraph performance-tested both approaches and determined that the fine-grained, property-free approach was nearly twice as fast as the one using properties. For more details on designing relationships, see Chapter 4.

Finding all accessible resources for an administrator

The TeleGraph application uses many different Cypher queries; we'll look at just a few of them here.

First up is the ability to find all the resources an administrator can access. Whenever an onsite administrator logs in to the system, he is presented with a browser-based list of all the employees and employee accounts he can administer. This list is generated based on the results returned from the following query:

```
START admin=node:administrator(name={administratorName})
MATCH paths=(admin)-[:MEMBER_OF]->()-[:ALLOWED_INHERIT]->()
         <-[:CHILD_OF*0..3]-(company)<-[:WORKS_FOR]-(employee)
         -[:HAS_ACCOUNT]->(account)
WHERE NOT ((admin)-[:MEMBER_OF]->()-[:DENIED]->()<-[:CHILD_OF*0..3]-(company))
RETURN employee.name AS employee, account.name AS account
UNION
START admin=node:administrator(name={administratorName})
MATCH paths=(admin)-[:MEMBER_OF]->()-[:ALLOWED_DO_NOT_INHERIT]->()
```

```
<-[:WORKS_FOR]-(employee)-[:HAS_ACCOUNT]->(account)
RETURN employee.name AS employee, account.name AS account
```

This query sets the template for all the other queries we'll be looking at in this section, in that it comprises two separate queries joined by a UNION operator, which was introduced with Neo4j 2.0. The query before the UNION operator handles ALLOWED_INHERIT relationships qualified by any DENIED relationships; the query following the UNION operator handles any ALLOWED_DO_NOT_INHERIT permissions. This pattern, ALLOWED_INHERIT minus DENIED, followed by ALLOWED_DO_NOT_INHERIT, is repeated in all of the access control example queries that follow.

The first query here, the one before the UNION operator, can be broken down as follows:

- START finds the logged-in administrator in the administrator index, and binds the result to the admin identifier.

- MATCH matches all the groups to which this administrator belongs, and from these groups, all the parent companies connected by way of an ALLOWED_INHERIT relationship. The MATCH then uses a variable-length path ([:CHILD_OF*0..3]) to discover children of these parent companies, and thereafter the employees and accounts associated with all matched companies (whether parent company or child). At this point, the query has matched all companies, employees, and accounts accessible by way of ALLOWED_INHERIT relationships.

- WHERE eliminates matches whose company, or parents, are connected by way of DENIED relationship to the administrator's groups. This WHERE clause is invoked for each match; if there is a DENIED relationship anywhere between the admin node and the company node bound by the match, that match is eliminated.

- RETURN creates a projection of the matched data in the form of a list of employee names and accounts.

The second query here, following the UNION operator, is a little simpler:

- The MATCH clause simply matches companies (plus employees and accounts) that are directly connected to an administrator's groups by way of an ALLOWED_DO_NOT_INHERIT relationship.

The UNION operator joins the results of these two queries together, eliminating any duplicates. Note that the RETURN clause in each query must contain the same projection of the results; in other words, the column names in the results must match.

Figure 5-9 shows how this query matches all accessible resources for Sarah in the sample TeleGraph graph. Note that, because of the DENIED relationship from Group 2 to Skunk workz, Sarah cannot administer Kate and Account 7.

Cypher supports both UNION and UNION ALL operators. UNION eliminates duplicate results from the final result set, whereas UNION ALL includes any duplicates.

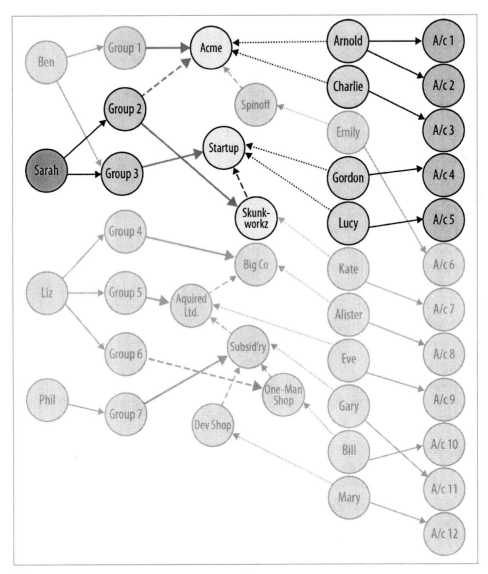

Figure 5-9. Finding all accessible resources for a user

Determining whether an administrator has access to a resource

The query we've just looked at returned a list of employees and accounts an administrator can manage. In a web application, each of these resources (employee, account) is accessible through its own URI. Given a friendly URI (e.g., *http://TeleGraph/accounts/5436*), what's to stop someone from hacking a URI and gaining illegal access to an account?

What's needed is a query that will determine whether an administrator has access to a specific resource. This is that query:

```
START admin=node:administrator(name={adminName}),
      company=node:company(resourceName={resourceName})
MATCH p=(admin)-[:MEMBER_OF]->()-[:ALLOWED_INHERIT]->()
        <-[:CHILD_OF*0..3]-(company)
WHERE NOT ((admin)-[:MEMBER_OF]->()-[:DENIED]->()
            <-[:CHILD_OF*0..3]-(company))
RETURN count(p) AS accessCount
UNION
START admin=node:administrator(name={adminName}),
      company=node:company(resourceName={resourceName})
MATCH p=(admin)-[:MEMBER_OF]->()-[:ALLOWED_DO_NOT_INHERIT]->(company)
RETURN count(p) AS accessCount
```

This query works by determining whether an administrator has access to the company to which an employee or an account belongs. How do we identify the company to which an employee or account belongs? Through clever use of indexes.

In the TeleGraph data model, companies are indexed both by their name, and by the names of their employees and employee accounts. Given a company name, employee name, or account name, we can, therefore, look up the relevant company node in the company index.

With that bit of insight, we can see that this resource authorization check is similar to the query for finding all companies, employees, and accounts—only with several small differences:

- company is bound in the START clause, not the MATCH clause. Using the indexing strategy described earlier, we look up the node representing the relevant company based on the name of the resource to be authorized—whether employee or account.

- We don't match any further than company. Because company has already been bound based on an employee or account name, there's no need to drill further into the graph to match that employee or account.

- The RETURN clauses for the queries before and after the UNION operator return a count of the number of matches. For an administrator to have access to a resource, one or both of these accessCount values must be greater than 0.

The WHERE clause in the query before the UNION operator once again eliminates matches where the company in question is connected to one of the administrator's groups by way of a DENIED relationship.

Because the UNION operator eliminates duplicate results, the overall result set for this query can contain either one or two values. The client-side logic for determining whether an administrator has access to a resource looks like this in Java:

```
private boolean isAuthorized( ExecutionResult result )
{
    Iterator<Long> accessCountIterator = result.columnAs( "accessCount" );
    while ( accessCountIterator.hasNext() )
    {
        if (accessCountIterator.next() > 0L)
        {
            return true;
        }
    }
    return false;
}
```

Finding administrators for an account

The previous two queries represent "top-down" views of the graph. The last TeleGraph query we'll discuss here provides a "bottom-up" view of the data. Given a resource—an employee or account—who can manage it? Here's the query:

```
START resource=node:resource(name={resourceName})
MATCH p=(resource)-[:WORKS_FOR|HAS_ACCOUNT*1..2]-(company)
        -[:CHILD_OF*0..3]->()<-[:ALLOWED_INHERIT]-()<-[:MEMBER_OF]-(admin)
WHERE NOT ((admin)-[:MEMBER_OF]->()-[:DENIED]->()<-[:CHILD_OF*0..3]-(company))
RETURN admin.name AS admin
UNION
START resource=node:resource(name={resourceName})
MATCH p=(resource)-[:WORKS_FOR|HAS_ACCOUNT*1..2]-(company)
        <-[:ALLOWED_DO_NOT_INHERIT]-()<-[:MEMBER_OF]-(admin)
RETURN admin.name AS admin
```

As before, the query consists of two independent queries joined by a UNION operator. Of particular note are the following clauses:

- The START clauses use a resource index, a named index for both employees and accounts.

- The MATCH clauses contain a variable-length path expression that uses the | operator to specify a path that is one or two relationships deep, and whose relationship types comprise WORKS_FOR and HAS_ACCOUNT. This expression accommodates the fact that the subject of the query may be either an employee or an account.

Figure 5-10 shows the portions of the graph matched by the query when asked to find the administrators for Account 10.

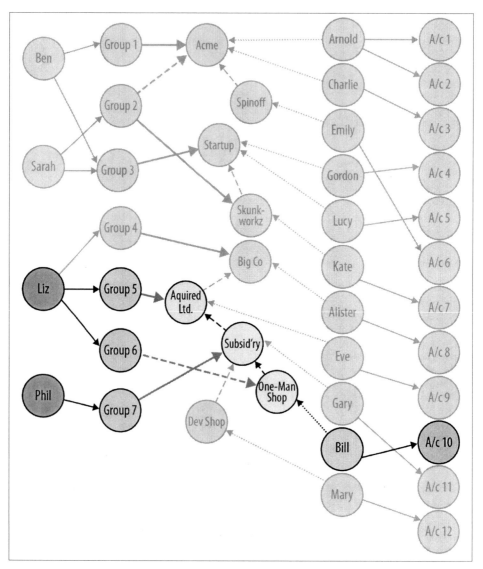

Figure 5-10. Finding an administrator for a specific account

Geo (Logistics)

Global Post is a global shipper whose domestic operation delivers millions of parcels to more than 30 million addresses each day. In recent years, as a result of the rise in Internet shopping, the number of parcels has increased significantly. Amazon and eBay deliveries now account for more than half the parcels routed and delivered by Global Post each day.

With parcel volumes continuing to grow, and facing strong competition from other courier services, Global Post has begun a large change program to upgrade all aspects of its parcel network, including buildings, equipment, systems, and processes.

One of the most important and time-critical components in the parcel network is the route calculation engine. Between one and three thousand parcels enter the network each second. As parcels enter the network they are mechanically sorted according to their destination. To maintain a steady flow during this process, the engine must calculate a parcel's route before it reaches a point where the sorting equipment has to make a choice, which happens only seconds after the parcel has entered the network—hence the strict time requirements on the engine.

Not only must the engine route parcels in milliseconds, but it must do so according to the routes scheduled for a particular period. Parcel routes change throughout the year, with more trucks, delivery people, and collections over the Christmas period than during the summer, for example. The engine must, therefore, apply its calculations using only those routes that are available for a particular period.

On top of accommodating different routes and levels of parcel traffic, the new parcel network must also allow for significant change and evolution. The platform that Global Post develops today will form the business-critical basis of its operations for the next 10 years or more. During that time, the company anticipates large portions of the network—including equipment, premises, and transport routes—will change to match changes in the business environment. The data model underlying the route calculation engine must, therefore, allow for rapid and significant schema evolution.

Global Post data model

Figure 5-11 shows a simple example of the Global Post parcel network. The network comprises parcel centers, which are connected to delivery bases, each of which covers several delivery areas; these delivery areas, in turn, are subdivided into delivery segments covering many delivery units. There are around 25 national parcel centers and roughly 2 million delivery units (corresponding to postal or zip codes).

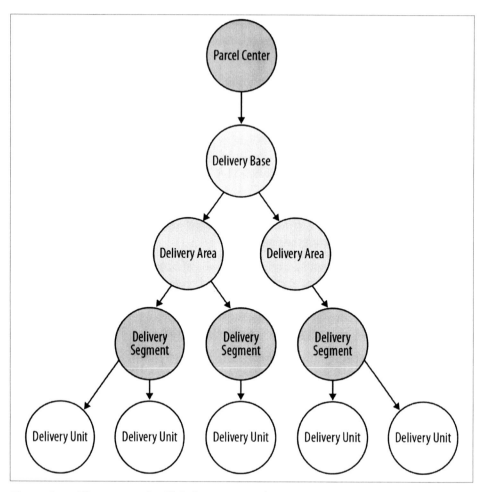

Figure 5-11. Elements in the Global Post network

Over time, the delivery routes change. Figure 5-12, Figure 5-13, and Figure 5-14 show three distinct delivery periods. For any given period, there is at most one route between a delivery base and any particular delivery area or segment. In contrast, there may be multiple routes between delivery bases and parcel centers. For any given point in time, therefore, the lower portions of the graph, the individual subgraphs below each delivery base, comprise simple tree structures, whereas the upper portions of the graph, made up of delivery bases and parcel centers, are more complexly structured.

Notice that delivery units are not included in the production data. This is because each delivery unit is always associated with the same delivery segments, irrespective of the period. Because of this invariant, it is possible to index each delivery segment by its many delivery units. To calculate the route to a particular delivery unit, the system need only actually calculate the route to its associated delivery segment, which can be recovered from the index using the delivery unit as a key. This optimization helps both reduce the size of the production graph, and reduce the number of traversals needed to calculate a route.

The production database contains the details of many different delivery periods, as shown in Figure 5-15. This multiperiod graph shows some of the overall complexity present in the data.

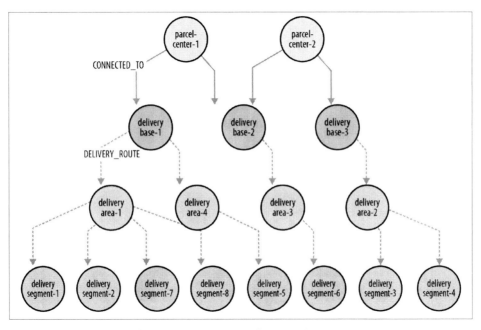

Figure 5-12. Structure of the delivery network for Period 1

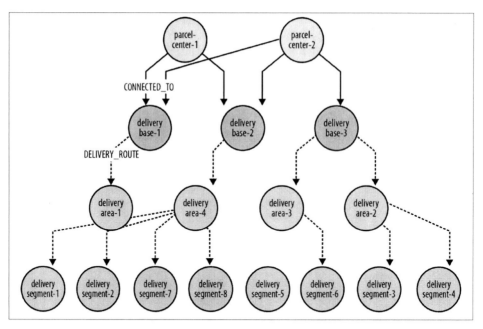

Figure 5-13. Structure of the delivery network for Period 2

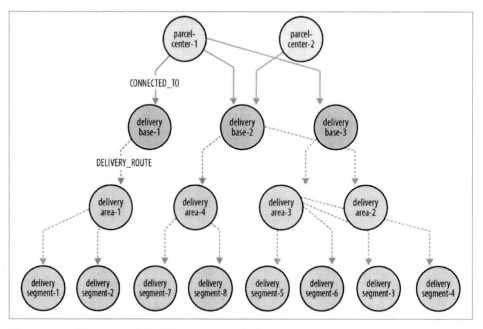

Figure 5-14. Structure of the delivery network for Period 3

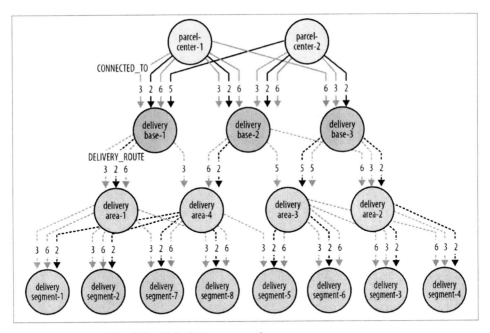

Figure 5-15. Sample of the Global Post network

In the production data, nodes are connected by multiple relationships, each of which is timestamped with a `start_date` and `end_date` property. Relationships are of two types: `CONNECTED_TO`, which connect parcel centers and delivery bases, and `DELIVERY_ROUTE`, which connect delivery bases to delivery areas, and delivery areas to delivery segments. These two different types of relationships effectively partition the graph into its upper and lower parts, which, as we'll see shortly, provides for efficient traversals. Figure 5-16 shows three of the timestamped `CONNECTED_TO` relationships connecting a parcel center to a delivery base.

Route calculation

As described in the previous section, the `CONNECTED_TO` and `DELIVERY_ROUTE` relationships partition the graph into *upper* and *lower* parts, with the upper parts made up of complexly connected parcel centers and delivery centers, the lower parts of delivery bases, delivery areas, and delivery segments organized—for any given period—in simple tree structures.

Route calculations involve finding the cheapest route between two locations in the lower portions of the graph. The starting location is typically a delivery segment or delivery area, whereas the end location is always a delivery segment (indexed, as we discussed earlier, by its delivery units). Irrespective of the start and end locations, the calculated route must go via at least one parcel center in the upper part of the graph.

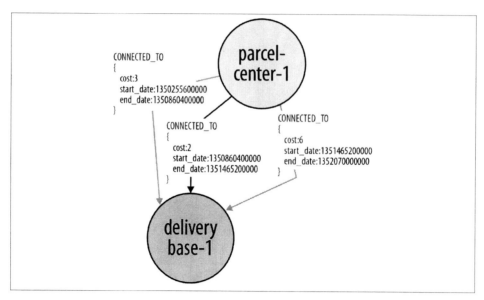

Figure 5-16. Timestamp properties on relationships

In terms of traversing the graph, a calculation can be split into three legs. Legs one and two, shown in Figure 5-17, work their way upward from the start and end locations, respectively, with each terminating at a delivery center. Because there is at most one route between any two elements in the lower portion of the graph for any given delivery period, traversing from one element to the next is simply a matter of finding an incoming DELIVERY ROUTE relationship whose interval timestamps *encompass* the current delivery period. By following these relationships, the traversals for legs one and two navigate a pair of tree structures rooted at two different delivery centers. These two delivery centers then form the start and end locations for the third leg, which crosses the upper portion of the graph.

As with legs one and two, the traversal for leg three, as shown in Figure 5-18, looks for relationships—this time, CONNECTED_TO relationships—whose timestamps *encompass* the current delivery period. Even with this time filtering in place, however, there are, for any given period, potentially several routes between any two delivery centers in the upper portion of the graph; thus the third leg traversal must sum the cost of each route, and select the cheapest, making this a *shortest weighted path* calculation.

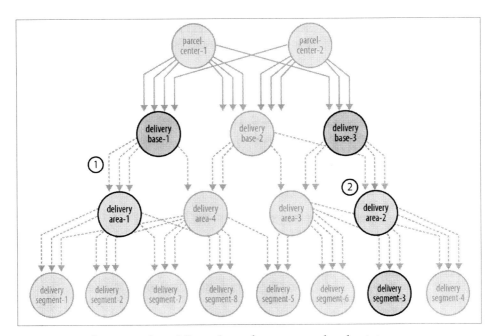

Figure 5-17. Shortest path to delivery bases from start and end points

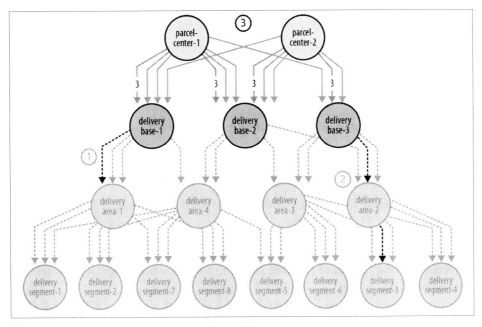

Figure 5-18. Shortest path between delivery bases

To complete the calculation, we need then simply add the paths for legs one, three, and two, which gives the full path from the start to the end location.

Finding the shortest delivery route using Cypher

The Cypher query to implement the parcel route calculation engine is as follows:

```
START s=node:location(name={startLocation}),
      e=node:location(name={endLocation})
MATCH upLeg = (s)<-[:DELIVERY_ROUTE*1..2]-(db1)
WHERE all(r in relationships(upLeg)
          WHERE r.start_date <= {intervalStart}
          AND r.end_date >= {intervalEnd})
WITH  e, upLeg, db1
MATCH downLeg = (db2)-[:DELIVERY_ROUTE*1..2]->(e)
WHERE all(r in relationships(downLeg)
          WHERE r.start_date <= {intervalStart}
          AND r.end_date >= {intervalEnd})
WITH  db1, db2, upLeg, downLeg
MATCH topRoute = (db1)<-[:CONNECTED_TO]-()-[:CONNECTED_TO*1..3]-(db2)
WHERE all(r in relationships(topRoute)
          WHERE r.start_date <= {intervalStart}
          AND r.end_date >= {intervalEnd})
WITH  upLeg, downLeg, topRoute,
      reduce(weight=0, r in relationships(topRoute) : weight+r.cost) AS score
      ORDER BY score ASC
      LIMIT 1
RETURN (nodes(upLeg) + tail(nodes(topRoute)) + tail(nodes(downLeg))) AS n
```

At first glance this query appears quite complex. It is, however, made up of four simpler queries joined together with WITH clauses. We'll look at each of these subqueries in turn.

Here's the first subquery:

```
START s=node:location(name={startLocation}),
      e=node:location(name={endLocation})
MATCH upLeg = (s)<-[:DELIVERY_ROUTE*1..2]-(db1)
WHERE all(r in relationships(upLeg)
          WHERE r.start_date <= {intervalStart}
          AND r.end_date >= {intervalEnd})
```

This query calculates the first leg of the overall route. It can be broken down as follows:

- START finds the start and end locations in an index, binding them to the s and e identifiers, respectively. (Remember, the endLocation lookup term describes a delivery unit, but the node returned from the location index represents a delivery segment.)

- MATCH finds the route from the start location, s, to a delivery base using a directed, variable-length DELIVERY_ROUTE path. This path is then bound to the identifier upLeg. Because delivery bases are always the root nodes of DELIVERY_ROUTE trees, and therefore have no incoming DELIVERY_ROUTE relationships, we can be confident that the db1 node at the end of this variable-length path represents a delivery base and not some other parcel network element.

- WHERE applies additional constraints to the path upLeg, ensuring that we only match DELIVERY_ROUTE relationships whose start_date and end_date properties encompass the supplied delivery period.

The second subquery calculates the second leg of the route, which comprises the path from the end location to another delivery center elsewhere in the network. This query is very similar to the first:

```
WITH  e, upLeg, db1
MATCH downLeg = (db2)-[:DELIVERY_ROUTE*1..2]->(e)
WHERE all(r in relationships(downLeg)
         WHERE r.start_date <= {intervalStart}
         AND r.end_date >= {intervalEnd})
```

The WITH clause here chains the first subquery to the second, piping the end location and the first leg's path and delivery base to the second subquery. The second subquery uses only the end location, e, in its MATCH clause; the rest is provided so that it can be piped to subsequent queries.

The third subquery identifies *all* candidate paths for the third leg of the route, as follows:

```
WITH  db1, db2, upLeg, downLeg
MATCH topRoute = (db1)<-[:CONNECTED_TO]-()-[:CONNECTED_TO*1..3]-(db2)
WHERE all(r in relationships(topRoute)
         WHERE r.start_date <= {intervalStart}
         AND r.end_date >= {intervalEnd})
```

This subquery is broken down as follows:

- WITH chains this subquery to the previous one, piping the delivery bases and paths identified in legs one and two to the current query.

- MATCH identifies *all* paths between the first and second leg delivery bases, to a maximum depth of four, and binds them to the topRoute identifier.

- WHERE constrains the topRoute paths to those whose start_date and end_date properties encompass the supplied delivery period.

The fourth and final subquery selects the shortest path for leg three, and then calculates the overall route:

```
WITH  upLeg, downLeg, topRoute,
      reduce(weight=0, r in relationships(topRoute) : weight+r.cost) AS score
      ORDER BY score ASC
      LIMIT 1
RETURN (nodes(upLeg) + tail(nodes(topRoute)) + tail(nodes(downLeg))) AS n
```

This subquery works as follows:

- WITH pipes one or more triples, comprising upLeg, downLeg, and topRoute, to the current query. There will be one triple for each of the paths matched by the third subquery, with each path being bound to topRoute in successive triples (the paths bound to upLeg and downLeg will stay the same, because the first and second subqueries matched only one path each). Each triple is accompanied by a score for the path bound to topRoute for that triple. This score is calculated using Cypher's reduce function, which for each triple sums the cost properties on the relationships in the path currently bound to topRoute; reduce was introduced with Neo4j 1.9. The triples are then ordered by this score, lowest first, and then limited to the first triple in the sorted list.

- RETURN sums the nodes in the paths upLeg, topRoute, and downLeg to produce the final results. The tail function drops the first node in each of paths topRoute and downLeg, because that node will already be present in the preceding path.

Implementing route calculation with the traversal framework

The time-critical nature of the route calculation coupled with the high throughput of the parcel network impose strict demands on the route calculation engine. As long as the individual query latencies are low enough, it's always possible to scale horizontally for increased throughput. The Cypher-based solution is fast, but with such high sustained throughput, every millisecond impacts the cluster footprint. For this reason, Global Post adopted an alternative approach: calculating routes using Neo4j's traversal framework.

A traversal-based implementation of the route calculation engine must solve two problems: finding shortest paths, and filtering paths based on time period. We'll look at filtering paths based on time period first.

Traversals should follow only relationships that are valid for the specified delivery period. In other words, as the traversal progresses through the graph, it should only be presented with relationships whose periods of validity, as defined by their start_date and end_date properties, contain the specified delivery period.

We implement this relationship filtering using a PathExpander. Given a path from a traversal's start node to the node where it is currently positioned, a PathExpander's expand() method returns the relationships that can be used to traverse further. This method is called by the traversal framework each time the framework advances another node into the graph. If needed, the client can supply some initial state that flows along each branch; expand() can then use (and even change) this state in the course of deciding which relationships to return. The route calculator's ValidPathExpander implementation uses this branch state to supply the delivery period to the expander.

Here's the code for the ValidPathExpander:

```
private static class IntervalPathExpander implements PathExpander<Interval>
{
  private final RelationshipType relationshipType;
  private final Direction direction;

  private IntervalPathExpander( RelationshipType relationshipType,
                                Direction direction )
  {
     this.relationshipType = relationshipType;
     this.direction = direction;
  }

  @Override
  public Iterable<Relationship> expand( Path path,
                                         BranchState<Interval> deliveryInterval )
  {
     List<Relationship> results = new ArrayList<Relationship>();
     for ( Relationship r : path.endNode()
                       .getRelationships( relationshipType, direction ) )
     {
        Interval relationshipInterval = new Interval(
               (Long) r.getProperty( "start_date" ),
               (Long) r.getProperty( "end_date" ) );
        if ( relationshipInterval.contains( deliveryInterval.getState() ) )
        {
           results.add( r );
        }
     }

     return results;
  }
}
```

The IntervalPathExpander's constructor takes two arguments: a relationshipType and a direction. This allows the expander to be reused for different types of relationships: in the case of the Global Post graph, the expander will be used to filter both CONNECTED_TO and DELIVERY_ROUTE relationships.

The expander's expand() method takes the path to the current node, and the deliveryInterval as supplied by the client. Each time it is called, expand() iterates the relevant relationships on the current node (the current node is given by path.endNode()). For each relationship, the method then compares the relationship's interval with the delivery interval. If the relationship's interval *contains* the delivery interval, the relationship is added to the results.

Having looked at the IntervalPathExpander, we can now turn to the ParcelRouteCalculator itself. This class encapsulates all the logic necessary to calculate a route between the point where a parcel enters the network and the final delivery destination. It employs a similar strategy to the Cypher query we've already looked at: it works its way up the graph from both the start node and the end node in two separate traversals, until it finds a delivery base for each leg. It then performs a shortest weighted path search that joins these two delivery bases.

Here's the beginning of the ParcelRouteCalculator class:

```
public class ParcelRouteCalculator
{
    private static final PathExpander<Interval> DELIVERY_ROUTE_EXPANDER =
            new IntervalPathExpander( withName( "DELIVERY_ROUTE" ),
                                      Direction.INCOMING );

    private static final PathExpander<Interval> CONNECTED_TO_EXPANDER =
            new IntervalPathExpander( withName( "CONNECTED_TO" ),
                                      Direction.BOTH );

    private static final TraversalDescription DELIVERY_BASE_FINDER =
        Traversal.description()
            .depthFirst()
            .evaluator( new Evaluator()
            {
                private final RelationshipType DELIVERY_ROUTE =
                    withName( "DELIVERY_ROUTE");

                @Override
                public Evaluation evaluate( Path path )
                {
                    if ( isDeliveryBase( path ) )
                    {
                        return Evaluation.INCLUDE_AND_PRUNE;
                    }

                    return Evaluation.EXCLUDE_AND_CONTINUE;
                }

                private boolean isDeliveryBase( Path path )
                {
                    return !path.endNode().hasRelationship(
                        DELIVERY_ROUTE, Direction.INCOMING );
                }
            } );

    private static final CostEvaluator<Double> COST_EVALUATOR =
            CommonEvaluators.doubleCostEvaluator( "cost" );

    private final Index<Node> locationIndex;

    public ParcelRouteCalculator( GraphDatabaseService db )
    {
        this.locationIndex = db.index().forNodes( "location" );
    }
```

```
        ...
    }
```

Here we define two expanders—one for DELIVERY_ROUTE relationships, another for CONNECTED_TO relationships—and the traversal that will find the two legs of our route. This traversal terminates whenever it encounters a node with no incoming DELIV ERY_ROUTE relationships. Because each delivery base is at the root of a delivery route tree, we can infer that a node without any incoming DELIVERY_ROUTE relationships represents a delivery base in our graph.

The constructor for ParcelRouteCalculator accepts the current database instance. From this it obtains the location index, which it stores in a member variable.

Each route calculation engine maintains a single instance of this route calculator. This instance is capable of servicing multiple requests. For each route to be calculated, the client calls the calculator's calculateRoute() method, passing in the names of the start and end points, and the interval for which the route is to be calculated:

```
public Iterable<Node> calculateRoute( String start,
                                      String end,
                                      Interval interval )
{
    TraversalDescription deliveryBaseFinder =
        createDeliveryBaseFinder( interval );

    Path upLeg = findRouteToDeliveryBase( start, deliveryBaseFinder );
    Path downLeg = findRouteToDeliveryBase( end, deliveryBaseFinder );

    Path topRoute = findRouteBetweenDeliveryBases(
        upLeg.endNode(),
        downLeg.endNode(),
        interval );

    return combineRoutes( upLeg, downLeg, topRoute );
}
```

calculateRoute() first obtains a deliveryBaseFinder for the specified interval, which it then uses to find the routes for the two legs. Next, it finds the route between the delivery bases at the top of each leg, these being the last nodes in each leg's path. Finally, it combines these routes to generate the final results.

The createDeliveryBaseFinder() helper method creates a traversal description configured with the supplied interval:

```
private TraversalDescription createDeliveryBaseFinder( Interval interval )
{
    return DELIVERY_BASE_FINDER.expand( DELIVERY_ROUTE_EXPANDER,
            new InitialBranchState.State<Interval>( interval, interval ) );
}
```

This traversal description is built by expanding the ParcelRouteCalculator's static DELIVERY_BASE_FINDER traversal description using the DELIVERY_ROUTE_EXPANDER. The branch state for the expander is initialized at this point with the interval supplied by the client. This enables us to use the same base traversal description instance (DE LIVERY_BASE_FINDER) for multiple requests. This base description is expanded and parameterized for each request.

Properly configured with an interval, the traversal description is then supplied to fin dRouteToDeliveryBase(), which looks up a starting node in the location index, and then executes the traversal:

```
private Path findRouteToDeliveryBase( String startPosition,
                                      TraversalDescription deliveryBaseFinder )
{
    Node startNode = locationIndex.get( "name", startPosition ).getSingle();
    return deliveryBaseFinder.traverse( startNode ).iterator().next();
}
```

That's the two legs taken care of. The last part of the calculation requires us to find the shortest path between the delivery bases at the top of each of the legs. calculate Route() takes the last node from each leg's path, and supplies these two nodes together with the client-supplied interval to findRouteBetweenDeliveryBases(). Here's the implementation of findRouteBetweenDeliveryBases():

```
private Path findRouteBetweenDeliveryBases( Node deliveryBase1,
                                            Node deliveryBase2,
                                            Interval interval )
{
    PathFinder<WeightedPath> routeBetweenDeliveryBasesFinder =
            GraphAlgoFactory.dijkstra(
                CONNECTED_TO_EXPANDER,
                new InitialBranchState.State<Interval>( interval, interval ),
                COST_EVALUATOR );

    return routeBetweenDeliveryBasesFinder
            .findSinglePath( deliveryBase1, deliveryBase2 );
}
```

Rather than use a traversal description to find the shortest route between two nodes, this method uses a shortest weighted path algorithm from Neo4j's graph algorithm library—in this instance, we're using the Dijkstra algorithm (see "Path-Finding with Dijkstra's Algorithm" on page 164 for more details of the Dijkstra algorithm). This algorithm is configured with ParcelRouteCalculator's static CONNECTED_TO_EXPANDER, which in turn is initialized with the client-supplied branch state interval. The algorithm is also configured with a cost evaluator (another static member), which simply identifies the property on a relationship representing that relationship's weight or cost. A call to findSinglePath on the Dijkstra path finder returns the shortest path between the two delivery bases.

That's the hard work done. All that remains is to join these routes to form the final results. This is relatively straightforward, the only wrinkle being that the down leg's path must be reversed before being added to the results (the leg was calculated from final destination upward, whereas it should appear in the results delivery base downward):

```
private Set<Node> combineRoutes( Path upLeg,
                                 Path downLeg,
                                 Path topRoute )
{
    LinkedHashSet<Node> results = new LinkedHashSet<Node>();
    results.addAll( IteratorUtil.asCollection( upLeg.nodes() ));
    results.addAll( IteratorUtil.asCollection( topRoute.nodes() ));
    results.addAll( IteratorUtil.asCollection( downLeg.reverseNodes() ));
    return results;
}
```

Summary

In this chapter we've looked at some common real-world use cases for graph databases, and described in detail three case studies that show how graph databases have been used to build a social network, implement access control, and manage complex logistics calculations.

In the next chapter we dive deeper into the internals of a graph database. In the concluding chapter we look at some analytical techniques and algorithms for processing graph data.

CHAPTER 6

Graph Database Internals

In this chapter we peek under the hood and discuss the implementation of graph databases, showing how they differ from other means of storing and querying complex, semi-structured, densely connected data. Although it is true that no single universal architecture pattern exists, even among graph databases, this chapter describes the most common architecture patterns and components you can expect to find inside a graph database.

We illustrate the discussion in this chapter using the Neo4j graph database, for several reasons. Neo4j is a graph database with native processing capabilities as well as native graph storage (see Chapter 1 for a discussion of native graph processing and storage). In addition to being the most common graph database in use at the time of writing, it has the transparency advantage of being open source, making it easy for the adventuresome reader to go a level deeper and inspect the code. Finally, it is a database the authors know well.

Native Graph Processing

We've discussed the property graph model several times throughout this book; by now you should be familiar with its notion of nodes connected by way of named and directed relationships, with both the nodes and relationships serving as containers for properties. Although the model itself is reasonably consistent across graph database implementations, there are numerous ways to encode and represent the graph in the database engine's main memory. Of the many different engine architectures, we say that a graph database has native processing capabilities if it exhibits a property called *index-free adjacency*.

A database engine that utilizes index-free adjacency is one in which each node maintains direct references to its adjacent nodes; each node, therefore acts as a micro-index of other nearby nodes, which is much cheaper than using global indexes. It means that query times are independent of the total size of the graph, and are instead simply proportional to the amount of the graph searched.

A nonnative graph database engine, in contrast, uses (global) indexes to link nodes together, as shown in Figure 6-1. These indexes add a layer of indirection to each traversal, thereby incurring greater computational cost. Proponents for native graph processing argue that index-free adjacency is crucial for fast, efficient graph traversals.

To understand why native graph processing is so much more efficient than graphs based on heavy indexing, consider the following. Depending on the implementation, index lookups could be *O(log n)* in algorithmic complexity versus *O(1)* for looking up immediate relationships. To traverse a network of *m* steps, the cost of the indexed approach, at *O(m log n)*, dwarfs the cost of *O(m)* for an implementation that uses index-free adjacency.

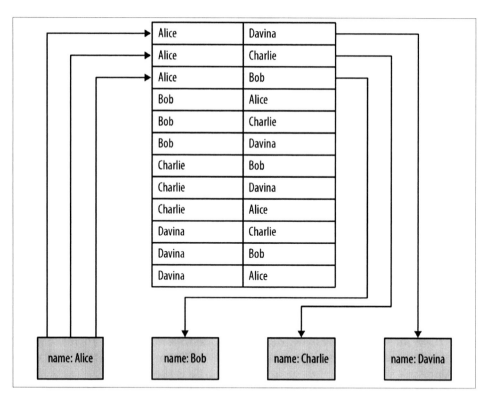

Figure 6-1. Nonnative graph processing engines use indexing to traverse between nodes

Figure 6-1 shows how a nonnative approach to graph processing works. To find Alice's friends we have first to perform an index lookup, at cost $O(\log n)$. This may be acceptable for occasional or shallow lookups, but it quickly becomes expensive when we reverse the direction of the traversal. If, instead of finding Alice's friends, we wanted to find out who is friends with Alice, we would have to perform multiple index lookups, one for each node that is potentially friends with Alice. This makes the cost far more onerous. Whereas it's $O(\log n)$ cost to find out who are Alice's friends, it's $O(m \log n)$ to find out who is friends with Alice.

Index-Free Adjacency Leads to Lower-Cost "Joins"

With index-free adjacency, bidirectional joins are effectively precomputed and stored in the database as relationships. In contrast, when using indexes to fake connections between records, there is no *actual* relationship stored in the database. This becomes problematic when we try to traverse in the "opposite" direction from the one for which the index was constructed. Because we have to perform a brute-force search through the index—which is an $O(n)$ operation—joins like this are simply too costly to be of any practical use.

Index lookups are fine for small networks, such as the one in Figure 6-1, but too costly for complex queries over larger graphs. Instead of using index lookups to make relationships concrete and navigable at query time, graph databases such as Neo4j with native graph processing capabilities use index-free adjacency to ensure high-performance traversals. Figure 6-2 shows how relationships eliminate the need for index lookups.

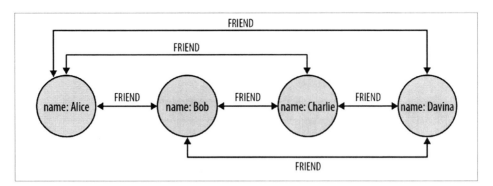

Figure 6-2. Neo4j uses relationships, not indexes, for fast traversals

Recall that in a general-purpose graph database relationships can be traversed in either direction (tail to head, or head to tail) extremely cheaply. As we see in Figure 6-2, to find Alice's friends using a graph, we simply follow her outgoing FRIEND relationships, at *O(1)* cost each. To find who is friends with Alice, we simply follow all of Alice's incoming FRIEND relationships to their source, again at *O(1)* cost each.

Given these costings, it's clear that, in theory at least, graph traversals can be very efficient. But such high-performance traversals only become reality when they are supported by an architecture designed for that purpose.

Native Graph Storage

If index-free adjacency is the key to high-performance traversals, queries, and writes, then one key aspect of the design of a graph database is the way in which graphs are stored. An efficient, native graph storage format supports extremely rapid traversals for arbitrary graph algorithms—an important reason for using graphs. For illustrative purposes we'll use the Neo4j database as an example of how a graph database is architected.

First, let's contextualize our discussion by looking at Neo4j's high-level architecture, presented in Figure 6-3. In what follows we'll work bottom-up, from the files on disk, through the programmatic APIs, and up to the Cypher query language. Along the way we'll discuss the performance and dependability characteristics of Neo4j, and the design decisions that make Neo4j a performant, reliable graph database.

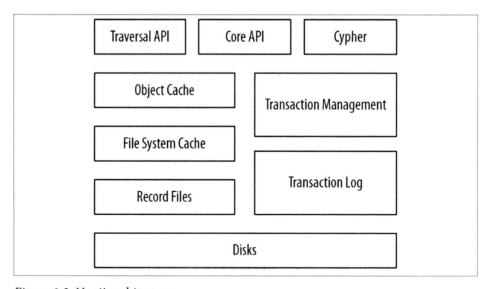

Figure 6-3. Neo4j architecture

Neo4j stores graph data in a number of different *store files*. Each store file contains the data for a specific part of the graph (e.g., nodes, relationships, properties). The division of storage responsibilities—particularly the separation of graph structure from property data—facilitates performant graph traversals, even though it means the user's view of their graph and the actual records on disk are structurally dissimilar. Let's start our exploration of physical storage by looking at the structure of nodes and relationships on disk as shown in Figure 6-4.

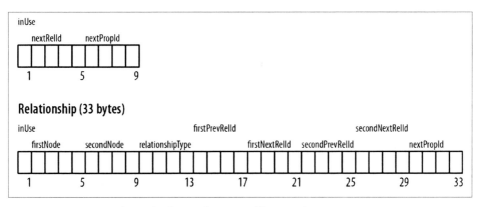

Figure 6-4. Neo4j node and relationship store file record structure

The node store file stores node records. Every node created in the user-level graph ends up in the node store, the physical file for which is `neostore.nodestore.db`. Like most of the Neo4j store files, the node store is a fixed-size record store, where each record is nine bytes in length. Fixed-size records enable fast lookups for nodes in the store file: if we have a node with id `100`, then we know its record begins 900 bytes into the file. Based on this format, the database can directly compute a record's location, at cost *O(1)*, rather than performing a search, which would be cost *O(log n)*.

The first byte of a node record is the in-use flag. This tells the database whether the record is currently being used to store a node, or whether it can be reclaimed on behalf of a new node (Neo4j's `.id` files keep track of unused records). The next four bytes represent the ID of the first relationship connected to the node, and the last four bytes represent the ID of the first property for the node. The node record is pretty lightweight: it's really just a couple of pointers to lists of relationships and properties.

Correspondingly, relationships are stored in the relationship store file, `neostore.rela` `tionshipstore.db`. Like the node store, the relationship store consists of fixed-sized records—in this case each record is 33 bytes long. Each relationship record contains the IDs of the nodes at the start and end of the relationship, a pointer to the relationship type (which is stored in the relationship type store), and pointers for the next and previous relationship records for each of the start and end nodes. These last pointers are part of what is often called the *relationship chain*.

The node and relationship stores are concerned only with the structure of the graph, not its property data. Both stores use fixed-sized records so that any individual record's location within a store file can be rapidly computed given its ID. These are critical design decisions that underline Neo4j's commitment to high-performance traversals.

In Figure 6-5 we see how the various store files interact on disk. Each of the two node records contains a pointer to that node's first property and first relationship in a relationship chain. To read a node's properties, we follow the singly linked list structure beginning with the pointer to the first property. To find a relationship for a node, we follow that node's relationship pointer to its first relationship (the LIKES relationship in this example). From here, we then follow the doubly linked list of relationships for that particular node (that is, either the start node doubly linked list, or the end node doubly linked list) until we find the relationship we're interested in. Having found the record for the relationship we want, we can read that relationship's properties (if there are any) using the same singly linked list structure as is used for node properties, or we can examine the node records for the two nodes the relationship connects using its start node and end node IDs. These IDs, multiplied by the node record size, give the immediate offset of each node in the node store file.

Doubly Linked Lists in the Relationship Store

Don't worry if the relationship store structure seems a little complex at first; it's definitely not as simple as the node store or property store.

It's helpful to think of a relationship record as "belonging" to two nodes—the start node and the end node of the relationship. Clearly, however, we don't want to store two relationship records, because that would be wasteful. And yet it's equally clear that the relationship record should somehow belong to both the start node and the end node.

That's why there are pointers (aka record IDs) for two doubly linked lists: one is the list of relationships visible from the start node; the other is the list of relationships visible from the end node. That each list is doubly linked simply enables us to rapidly iterate through that list in either direction, and insert and delete relationships efficiently.

Choosing to follow a different relationship involves iterating through a linked list of relationships until we find a good candidate (e.g., matching the correct type, or having some matching property value). Once we have a suitable relationship we're back in business, multiplying ID by record size, and thereafter chasing pointers.

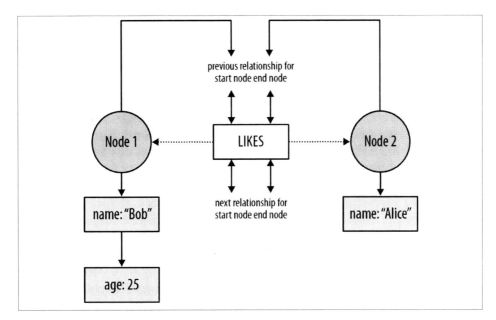

Figure 6-5. How a graph is physically stored in Neo4j

With fixed-sized records and pointer-like record IDs, traversals are implemented simply by chasing pointers around a data structure, which can be performed at very high speed. To traverse a particular relationship from one node to another, the database performs several cheap ID computations (these computations are much cheaper than searching global indexes, as we'd have to do if faking a graph in a nongraph native database):

1. From a given node record, locate the first record in the relationship chain by computing its offset into the relationship store—that is, by multiplying its ID by the fixed relationship record size (remember, that's 33 bytes at the time of writing). This gets us directly to the right record in the relationship store.

2. From the relationship record, look in the *second node* field to find the ID of the second node. Multiply that ID by the node record size (nine bytes at the time of writing) to locate the correct node record in the store.

Should we wish to constrain the traversal to relationships with particular types, then we'd add a lookup in the relationship type store. Again this is a simple multiplication of ID by record size (five bytes at the time of writing) to find the offset for the appropriate relationship type record in the relationship store.

In addition to the node and relationship stores, which contain the graph structure, we have the property store files. These store the user's key-value pairs. Recall that Neo4j, being a property graph database, allows properties—name-value pairs—to be attached to both nodes and relationships. The property stores, therefore, are referenced from both node and relationship records.

Records in the property store are physically stored in the `neostore.propertys tore.db` file. As with the node and relationship stores, property records are of a fixed size. Each property record consists of four property blocks and the ID of the next property in the property chain (remember, properties are held as a singly linked list on disk as compared to the doubly linked list used in relationship chains). Each property occupies between one and four property blocks—a property record can, therefore, hold a maximum of four properties. A property record holds the property type (Neo4j allows any primitive JVM type, plus strings, plus arrays of the JVM primitive types), and a pointer to the property index file (`neostore.propertystore.db.index`), which is where the property name is stored. For each property's value, the record contains either a pointer into a dynamic store record or an inlined value. The dynamic stores allow for storing large property values. There are two dynamic stores: a dynamic string store (`neostore.propertystore.db.strings`) and a dynamic array store (`neostore.prop ertystore.db.arrays`). Dynamic records comprise linked lists of fixed-sized records; a very large string, or large array, may, therefore, occupy more than one dynamic record.

Inlining and Optimizing Property Store Utilization

Neo4j supports store optimizations, whereby it inlines some properties into the property store file directly (`neostore.propertystore.db`). This happens when property data can be encoded to fit in one or more of a record's four property blocks. In practice this means that data like phone numbers and zip codes can be inlined in the property store file directly, rather than being pushed out to the dynamic stores. This results in reduced I/O operations and improved throughput, because only a single file access is required.

In addition to inlining certain compatible property values, Neo4j also maintains space discipline on property names. For example, in a social graph, there will likely be many nodes with properties like `first_name` and `last_name`. It would be wasteful if each property name was written out to disk verbatim, and so instead property names are indirectly referenced from the property store through the property index file. The property index allows all properties with the same name to share a single record, and thus for repetitive graphs—a very common use case—Neo4j achieves considerable space and I/O savings.

Having an efficient storage layout is only half the picture. Despite the store files having been optimized for rapid traversals, hardware considerations can still have a significant impact on performance. Memory capacity has increased significantly in recent years; nonetheless, very large graphs will still exceed our ability to hold them entirely in main memory. Spinning disks have millisecond seek times in the order of single digits, which, though fast by human standards, are ponderously slow in computing terms. Solid State Disks (SSDs) are far better (because there's no significant seek penalty waiting for platters to rotate), but the path between CPU and disk is still more latent than the path to L2 cache or main memory, which is where ideally we'd like to operate on our graph.

To mitigate the performance characteristics of mechanical/electronic mass storage devices, many graph databases use in-memory caching to provide probabilistic low-latency access to the graph. Neo4j uses a two-tiered caching architecture to provide this functionality.

The lowest tier in the Neo4j caching stack is the *filesystem cache*. The filesystem cache is a page-affined cache, meaning the cache divides each store into discrete regions, and then holds a fixed number of regions per store file. The actual amount of memory to be used to cache the pages for each store file can be fine-tuned, though in the absence of input from the user, Neo4j will use sensible default values based on the capacity of the underlying hardware (*http://docs.neo4j.org/chunked/stable/configuration-caches.html*). Pages are evicted from the cache based on a Least Frequently Used (LFU) cache policy. Neo4j's default implementation leaves it up to the underlying operating system's memory-mapped filesystem to decide which pages to evict; that is, the operating system itself determines which segments of virtual memory to hold in real memory and which to flush out to disk.

The filesystem cache is particularly beneficial when related parts of the graph are modified at the same time such that they occupy the same page. This is a common pattern for writes, where we tend to persist whole subgraphs to disk in a single operation, rather than discrete nodes and relationships.

If the filesystem cache reflects the characteristics of typical write usage, the *high-level* or *object* cache is all about optimizing for arbitrary read patterns. The high-level cache stores object representations of nodes, relationships, and properties for rapid, in-memory graph traversal. Nodes in the object cache contain both properties and references to their relationships, making them much richer than their store file representations, and bringing them much more in line with what we expect as programmers. Conversely, relationship objects are much simpler, containing only their properties. A node's relationships are grouped by relationship type and direction; these groupings provide for fast lookups of specific relationships based on these characteristics. As with the underlying stores, all lookups are by ID, meaning they are very performant, as we see in Figure 6-6.

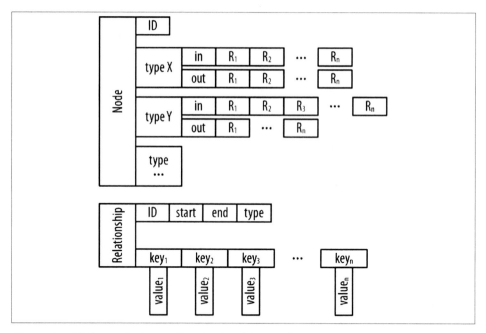

Figure 6-6. Nodes and relationships in the object cache

Programmatic APIs

Although the filesystem and caching infrastructures are fascinating in themselves, developers rarely interact with them directly; instead, developers manipulate a graph database through a query language, which can be either imperative or declarative. The examples in this book use the Cypher query language, the declarative query language native to Neo4j, because it is an easy language to learn and use. Other APIs exist, however, and depending on what we are doing, we may need to prioritize different concerns. It's important to understand the choice of APIs and their capabilities when embarking on a new project. If there is any one thing to take away from this section, it is the notion that these APIs can be thought of as a stack, as depicted in Figure 6-7: at the top we prize expressiveness and declarative programming; at the bottom we prize precision, imperative style, and (at the lowest layer) "bare metal" performance.

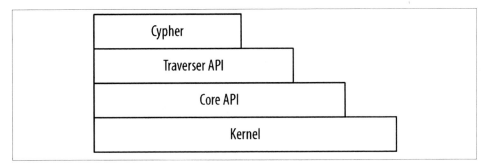

Figure 6-7. Logical view of the user-facing APIs in Neo4j

We discussed Cypher in some detail in Chapter 3. In the following sections we'll step through the remaining APIs from the bottom to the top. Again, these APIs are meant to be illustrative. Not all graph databases have the same number of layers, nor necessarily layers that behave and interact in precisely the same way. Each API has its advantages and disadvantages, which you should investigate so you can make an informed decision.

Kernel API

At the lowest level of the API stack are the kernel's transaction event handlers (*http://docs.neo4j.org/chunked/stable/transactions-events.html*). These allow user code to listen to transactions as they flow through the kernel, and thereafter to react (or not) based on the data content and lifecycle stage of the transaction.

Kernel Transaction Event Handlers

A typical use case for transaction event handlers is to prevent physical deletion of records. A handler can be set up to intercept deletion of a node and instead simply mark that node as logically deleted (or in a more sophisticated manner, move the node "back in time" by creating timestamped archive relationships).

Core (or "Beans") API

Neo4j's Core API is an imperative Java API that exposes the graph primitives of nodes, relationships, and properties to the user. When used for reads, the API is lazily evaluated, meaning that relationships are only traversed as and when the calling code demands the next node. Data is retrieved from the graph as quickly as the API caller can consume it, with the caller having the option to terminate the traversal at any point. For writes, the Core API provides transaction management capabilities to ensure atomic, consistent, isolated, and durable persistence.

In the following code, we see a snippet of code borrowed from the Neo4j tutorial (*https:// github.com/jimwebber/neo4j-tutorial*) in which we try to find human companions from the *Doctor Who* universe:[1]

```
// Index lookup for the node representing the doctor is omitted for brevity

Iterable<Relationship> relationships =
            doctor.getRelationships( Direction.INCOMING, COMPANION_OF );

for ( Relationship rel : relationships )
{
    Node companionNode = rel.getStartNode();
    if ( companionNode.hasRelationship( Direction.OUTGOING, IS_A ) )
    {
        Relationship singleRelationship = companionNode
                                        .getSingleRelationship( IS_A,
                                            Direction.OUTGOING );
        Node endNode = singleRelationship.getEndNode();
        if ( endNode.equals( human ) )
        {
            // Found one!
        }
    }
}
```

This code is very imperative: we simply loop round the Doctor's companions and check to see if any of the companion nodes have an IS_A relationship to the node representing the human species. If the companion node is connected to the human species node, we do something with it.

Because it is an imperative API, the Core API requires us to fine-tune it to the underlying graph structure. This can be very fast; at the same time, however, it means we end up baking knowledge of our specific domain structure into our code. Compared to the higher-level APIs (particularly Cypher) more code is needed to achieve an equivalent goal. Nonetheless, the affinity between the Core API and the underlying record store is plain to see—the structures used at the store and cache level are exposed relatively faithfully by the Core API to user code.

Traversal API

The Traversal API is a declarative Java API. It enables the user to specify a set of constraints that limit the parts of the graph the traversal is allowed to visit. We can specify which relationship types to follow, and in which direction (effectively specifying relationship filters); we can indicate whether we want the traversal to be performed breadth-first or depth-first; and we can specify a user-defined path evaluator that is triggered

---

1. *Doctor Who* is the world's longest-running science fiction show and a firm favorite of the Neo4j team.

with each node encountered. At each step of the traversal, this evaluator determines how the traversal is to proceed next. The following code snippet shows the Traversal API in action:

```
Traversal.description()
  .relationships( DoctorWhoRelationships.PLAYED, Direction.INCOMING )
  .breadthFirst()
  .evaluator( new Evaluator()
  {
    public Evaluation evaluate( Path path )
    {
      if ( path.endNode().hasRelationship(
                            DoctorWhoRelationships.REGENERATED_TO ) )
      {
        return Evaluation.INCLUDE_AND_CONTINUE;
      }
      else
      {
        return Evaluation.EXCLUDE_AND_CONTINUE;
      }
    }
  } );
```

With this snippet it's plain to see the predominantly declarative nature of the Traversal API. The `relationships()` method declares that only `PLAYED` relationships in the `IN COMING` direction may be traversed; thereafter, we declare that the traversal should be executed in a `breadthFirst()` manner, meaning it will visit all nearest neighbors before going further outward.

The Traversal API is declarative for graph structure; for our implementation of the `Evaluator`, however, we drop down to the imperative Core API. Within the evaluator we use the Core API to determine, given the path to the current node, whether or not further hops through the graph are necessary (we can also use the Core API to modify the graph from inside an evaluator). Again, the native graph structures inside the database bubble close to the surface here, with the graph primitives of nodes, relationships, and properties taking center stage in the API.

Core API, Traversal Framework, or Cypher?

Given these several different methods for querying a graph, which should we choose?

The Core API allows developers to fine-tune their queries so that they exhibit high affinity with the underlying graph. A well-written Core API query is often faster than any other approach. The downside is that such queries can be verbose, requiring considerable developer effort. Moreover, their high affinity with the underlying graph makes them tightly coupled to its structure: when the graph structure changes, they can often break. Cypher can be more tolerant of structural changes—things such as variable-length paths help mitigate variation and change.

The Traversal Framework is both more loosely coupled than the Core API (because it allows the developer to declare informational goals), and less verbose, and as a result a query written using the Traversal Framework typically requires less developer effort than the equivalent written using the Core API. Because it is a general-purpose framework, however, the Traversal Framework tends to perform marginally less well than a well-written Core API query.

If we find ourselves in the unusual situation of coding with the Core API or Traversal Framework (and thus eschewing Cypher and its affordances), it's because we are working on an edge case where we need to finely craft an algorithm that cannot be expressed effectively using Cypher's pattern matching. Choosing between the Core API and the Traversal Framework is a matter of deciding whether the higher abstraction/lower coupling of the Traversal Framework is sufficient, or whether the close-to-the-metal/higher coupling of the Core API is in fact necessary for implementing an algorithm correctly and in accordance with our performance requirements.

This concludes our brief survey of graph programming APIs, using the native Neo4j APIs as an example. We've seen how these APIs reflect the structures used in the lower levels of the Neo4j stack, and how this alignment permits for idiomatic and rapid graph traversals.

It's not enough for a database to be fast, however; it must also be dependable. This brings us to a discussion of the nonfunctional characteristics of graph databases.

Nonfunctional Characteristics

At this point we've understood what it means to construct a native graph database, and have seen how some of these graph-native capabilities are implemented, using Neo4j as our example. But to be considered *dependable*, any data storage technology must provide some level of guarantee as to the durability and accessibility of the stored data.[2]

One common measure by which relational databases are traditionally evaluated is the number of transactions per second they can process. In the relational world, it is assumed that these transactions uphold the ACID properties (even in the presence of failures) such that data is consistent and recoverable. For nonstop processing and managing of large volumes, a relational database is expected to scale so that many instances are available to process queries and updates, with the loss of an individual instance not unduly affecting the running of the cluster as a whole.

At a high level at least, much the same applies to graph databases: they need to guarantee consistency, recover gracefully from crashes, and prevent data corruption; further, they

---

2. The formal definition of dependability is the "trustworthiness of a computing system, which allows reliance to be justifiably placed on the service it delivers" as per *http://www.dependability.org/*.

need to scale out to provide high availability, and scale up for performance. In the following sections we'll explore what each of these requirements means for a graph database architecture. Once again, we'll expand on certain points by delving into Neo4j's architecture, as a means of providing concrete examples. It should be pointed out that not all graph databases are fully ACID. It is important, therefore, to understand the specifics of the transaction model of your chosen database. Neo4j's ACID transactionality shows the considerable levels of dependability that can be obtained from a graph database—levels we are accustomed to obtaining from enterprise-class relational database management systems.

Transactions

Transactions have been a bedrock of dependable computing systems for decades. Although many NOSQL stores are not transactional, in part because there's an unvalidated assumption that transactional systems scale less well, transactions remain a fundamental abstraction for dependability in contemporary graph databases—including Neo4j. (There is some truth to the claim that transactions limit scalability, insofar as distributed two-phase commit can exhibit unavailability problems in pathological cases, but in general the effect is much less marked than is often assumed.)

Transactions in Neo4j are semantically identical to traditional database transactions. Writes occur within a transaction context, with write locks being taken for consistency purposes on any nodes and relationships involved in the transaction. On successful *completion* of the transaction, changes are flushed to disk for durability, and the write locks released. These actions maintain the atomicity guarantees of the transaction. Should the transaction fail for some reason, the writes are discarded and the write locks released, thereby maintaining the graph in its previous consistent state.

Should two or more transactions attempt to change the same graph elements concurrently, Neo4j will detect a potential deadlock situation, and serialize the transactions. Writes within a single transactional context will not be visible to other transactions, thereby maintaining isolation.

How Transactions Are Implemented in Neo4j

The transaction implementation in Neo4j is conceptually straightforward. Each transaction is represented as an in-memory object whose state represents writes to the database. This object is supported by a lock manager, which applies write locks to nodes and relationships as they are created, updated, and deleted. On transaction rollback, the transaction object is simply discarded and the write locks released, whereas on successful completion the transaction is committed to disk.

Committing data to disk in Neo4j uses a *Write Ahead Log*, whereby changes are appended as actionable entries in the active transaction log. On transaction *commit*

(assuming a positive response to the *prepare* phase) a commit entry will be written to the log. This causes the log to be flushed to disk, thereby making the changes durable. Once the disk flush has occurred, the changes are applied to the graph itself. After all the changes have been applied to the graph, any write locks associated with the transaction are released.

Once a transaction has committed, the system is in a state where changes are guaranteed to be in the database even if a fault then causes a non-pathological failure. This, as we shall now see, confers substantial advantages for recoverability, and hence for ongoing provision of service.

Recoverability

Databases are no different from any other pieces of software in that they are susceptible to bugs in their implementation, in the hardware they run on, and in that hardware's power and cooling infrastructures. Though diligent engineers try to minimize the possibility of failure in all of these, at some point it's inevitable that a database will crash— though the mean time between failures should be very long indeed.

In a well-designed system, a database server crash, though annoying, ought not affect availability, though it may affect throughput. And when a failed server resumes operation, it must not serve corrupt data to its users, irrespective of the nature or timing of the crash.

When recovering from an unclean shutdown, perhaps caused by a fault or even an overzealous operator, Neo4j checks in the most recently active transaction log and replays any transactions it finds against the store. It's possible that some of those transactions *may* have already been applied to the store, but because replaying is an idempotent action, the net result is the same: after recovery, the store will be consistent with all transactions successfully committed prior to the failure.

Local recovery is all that is necessary in the case of a single database instance. Generally, however, we run databases in clusters (which we'll discuss shortly) to assure high availability on behalf of client applications. Fortunately, clustering confers additional benefits to recovering instances: not only will an instance become consistent with all transactions successfully committed prior to its failure, as discussed earlier, it can also quickly catch up with other instances in the cluster, and thereby be consistent with all transactions successfully committed *subsequent* to its failure. That is, once local recovery has completed, a replica can ask other members of the cluster—typically the master—for any newer transactions; it can then apply these newer transactions to its own dataset via transaction replay.

Recoverability deals with the capability of the database to set things right after a fault has arisen. In addition to recoverability, a good database needs to be highly available to meet the increasingly sophisticated needs of data-heavy applications.

Availability

In addition to being valuable in and of themselves, Neo4j's transaction and recovery capabilities also benefit its high-availability characteristics; its ability to recognize and, if necessary, repair an instance after crashing means that data quickly becomes available again without human intervention. And of course, more live instances increases the overall availability of the database to process queries.

It's uncommon to want individual disconnected database instances in a typical production scenario. More often, we cluster database instances for high availability. Neo4j uses a master-slave cluster arrangement to ensure a complete replica of the graph is stored on each machine. Writes are replicated out from the master to the slaves at frequent intervals. At any point, the master and some slaves will have a completely up-to-date copy of the graph, while other slaves will be catching up (typically, they will be but milliseconds behind).

For writes, the classic write-master with read-slaves is a popular topology. With this setup, all database writes are directed at the master, and read operations are directed at slaves. This provides asymptotic scalability for writes (up to the capacity of a single spindle) but allows for near linear scalability for reads (accounting for the modest overhead in managing the cluster).

Although write-master with read-slaves is a classic deployment topology, Neo4j also supports writing through slaves. In this scenario, the slave to which a write has been directed by the client first ensures it is consistent with the master (it "catches up"); thereafter, the write is synchronously transacted across both instances. This is useful when we want immediate durability in two database instances; furthermore, because it allows writes to be directed to any instance, it offers additional deployment flexibility. It comes at the cost of higher write latency, however, owing to the forced catchup phase. It does *not* imply that writes are distributed around the system: all writes must still pass through the master at some point.

Other Replication Options in Neo4j

In Neo4j version 1.8 onward it's possible to specify that writes to the master are replicated in a best-effort manner to an arbitrary number of replicas before a transaction is considered complete. This provides an alternative to the "at least two" level of durability achieved by writing through slaves. See "Replication" on page 79 for more details.

Another aspect of availability is contention for access to resources. An operation that contends for exclusive access (e.g., for writes) to a particular part of the graph may suffer from sufficiently high latency as to appear unavailable. We've seen similar contention with coarse-grained table-level locking in RDBMSs, where writes are latent even when there's logically no contention.

Fortunately, in a graph access patterns tend to be more evenly spread, especially where idiomatic graph-local queries are executed. A graph-local operation is one that starts at one or more given places in the graph and then traverses the surrounding subgraphs from there. The starting points for such queries tend to be things that are especially significant in the domain, such as users or products. These starting points result in the overall query load being distributed with low contention. In turn, clients perceive greater responsiveness and higher availability.

The Benefits of Idiomatic Queries

Jackie Stewart, the Formula 1 racing driver, is reputed to have said that to drive a car well you don't need to be an engineer but you do need mechanical sympathy. That is, the best performance comes as a result of the driver and car working together harmoniously.

In much the same way, graph database queries are considered mechanically sympathetic to the database when they are framed as idiomatic, graph-local queries that begin their traversal from one or more start points. The underlying infrastructure, including caching and store access, is optimized to support this kind of workload.

Idiomatic queries have beneficial side effects. For example, because caching is aligned with idiomatic searches, queries that are themselves idiomatic tend to exploit caches better and run faster than nonidiomatic queries. In turn, queries that run fast free up the database to run more of them, which means higher throughput and the sense of better availability from the client's point of view because there's less waiting around.

Unidiomatic queries (e.g., those which pick random nodes/relationships rather than traversing) exhibit the opposite characteristics: they disrespect the underlying caching layers and therefore run more slowly because more disk I/O is needed. Because the queries run slowly, the database can process fewer of them per second, which means the availability of the database to do useful work diminishes from the client's point of view.

Whatever the database, understanding the underlying storage and caching infrastructure will help us construct idiomatic—and hence, mechanically sympathetic—queries that maximize performance.

Our final observation on availability is that scaling for cluster-wide replication has a positive impact, not just in terms of fault-tolerance, but also responsiveness. Because there are many machines available for a given workload, query latency is low and availability is maintained. But as we'll now discuss, scale itself is more nuanced than simply the number of servers we deploy.

Scale

The topic of scale has become more important as data volumes have grown. In fact, the problems of data at scale, which have proven difficult to solve with relational databases, have been a substantial motivation for the NOSQL movement. In some sense, graph databases are no different; after all, they also need to scale to meet the workload demands of modern applications. But scale isn't a simple value like transactions per second: it's an aggregate value that we measure across multiple axes.

For graph databases, we will decompose our broad discussion on scale into three key themes:

1. Capacity (graph size)
2. Latency (response time)
3. Read and write throughput

Capacity

Some graph database vendors have chosen to eschew any upper bounds in graph size in exchange for performance and storage cost. Neo4j has taken a somewhat unique approach historically, having maintained a "sweet spot" that achieves faster performance and lower storage (and consequently diminished memory footprint and IO-ops) by optimizing for graph sizes that lie at or below the 95th percentile of use cases. The reason for the trade-off lies in the use of fixed record sizes and pointers, which (as discussed in "Native Graph Storage" on page 144) it uses extensively inside of the store. At the time of writing, the 1.9 release of Neo4j can support single graphs having tens of billions of nodes, relationships, and properties. This allows for graphs with a social networking dataset roughly the size of Facebook's.

 The Neo4j team has publicly expressed the intention to support 100B+ nodes/relationships/properties in a single graph as part of its 2013 roadmap.

How large must a dataset be to take advantage of all of the benefits a graph database has to offer? The answer is, smaller than you might think. For queries of second or third degree, the performance benefits show with datasets having a few single-digit thousand nodes. The higher the degree of the query, the more extreme the delta. The ease-of-development benefits are of course unrelated to data volume, and available regardless of the database size. The authors have seen meaningful production applications range from as small as a few tens of thousands of nodes, and a few hundred thousand relationships, to billions of nodes and relationships.

Latency

Graph databases don't suffer the same latency problems as traditional relational databases, where the more data we have in tables—and in indexes—the longer the join operations (this simple fact of life is one of the key reasons that performance tuning is nearly always the very top issue on a relational DBA's mind). With a graph database, most queries follow a pattern whereby an index is used simply to find a starting node (or nodes); the remainder of the traversal then uses a combination of pointer chasing and pattern matching to search the data store. What this means is that, unlike relational databases, performance does not depend on the total size of the dataset, but only on the data being queried. This leads to performance times that are nearly constant (i.e., are related to the size of the result set), even as the size of the dataset grows (though as we discussed in Chapter 3, it's still sensible to tune the structure of the graph to suit the queries, even if we're dealing with lower data volumes).

Throughput

We might think a graph database would need to scale in the same way as other databases. But this isn't the case. When we look at IO-intensive application behaviors, we see that a single complex business operation typically reads and writes a set of related data. In other words, the application performs multiple operations on a logical subgraph within the overall dataset. With a graph database such multiple operations can be rolled up into larger, more cohesive operations. Further, with a graph-native store, executing each operation takes less computational effort than the equivalent relational operation. Graphs scale by doing less work for the same outcome.

For example, imagine a publishing scenario in which we'd like to read the latest piece from an author. In a RDBMS we typically select the author's works by joining the authors table to a table of publications based on matching author ID, and then ordering the publications by publication date and limiting to the newest handful. Depending on the characteristics of the ordering operation, that might be a $O(log(n))$ operation, which isn't so very bad.

However, as shown in Figure 6-8, the equivalent graph operation is $O(1)$, meaning constant performance irrespective of dataset size. With a graph we simply follow the outbound relationship called WROTE from the author to the work at the head of a list (or tree) of published articles. Should we wish to find older publications, we simply follow the PREV relationships and iterate through a linked list (or, alternatively, recurse through a tree). Writes follow suit because we always insert new publications at the head of the list (or root of a tree), which is another constant time operation. This compares favorably to the RDBMS alternative, particularly because it naturally maintains constant time performance for reads.

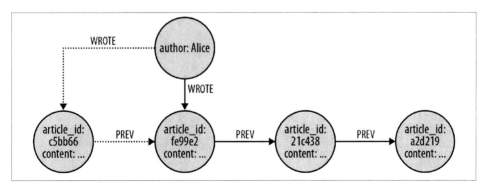

Figure 6-8. Constant time operations for a publishing system

Of course, there'll always be situations in which a single machine won't have sufficient I/O throughput to serve all the queries directed to it. When that happens, it's straightforward with Neo4j to build a cluster that scales horizontally for high availability and high read throughput. For typical workloads, where reads outstrip writes, this solution architecture can be ideal.

Should we exceed the capacity of a cluster, we can spread a graph across database instances by building *sharding* logic into the application. Sharding involves the use of a synthetic identifier to join records across database instances at the application level. How well this will perform depends very much on the shape of the graph. Some graphs lend themselves very well to this. Mozilla, for instance, uses the Neo4j graph database as part of its next-generation cloud browser, Pancake. Rather than having a single large graph, it stores a large number of small independent graphs, each tied to an end user. This makes it very easy to scale with no performance penalty.

Of course not all graphs have such convenient boundaries. If our graph is large enough that it needs to be broken up, but no natural boundaries exist, the approach we use is much the same as what we would use with a NOSQL store like MongoDB: we create synthetic keys, and relate records via the application layer using those keys plus some application-level resolution algorithm. The main difference from the MongoDB approach is that a native graph database will provide you with a performance boost anytime you are doing traversals within a database instance, whereas those parts of the traversal that run between instances will run at roughly the same speed as a MongoDB join. Overall performance should be markedly faster, however.

The Holy Grail of Graph Scalability

The eventual aim of most graph databases is to be able to partition a graph across many machines without application-level intervention so that access to the graph can be scaled horizontally. In the general case this is known to be an NP Hard problem, and thus impractical to solve. This manifests itself in graph databases as unpredictable query times as a result of traversals unexpectedly jumping between machines over a relatively slow network. However, there is innovation happening in this space, with triple stores able to scale horizontally very well (at the expense of latency); some nonnative graph stores piggy-backing onto other databases (like Twitter's FlockDB, which runs atop MySQL); and Neo4j's own horizontally scalable solution. This is certainly an exciting time to be in the data space.

Summary

In this chapter we've shown how property graphs are an excellent choice for pragmatic data modeling. We've explored the architecture of a graph database, with particular reference to the architecture of Neo4j, and discussed the nonfunctional characteristics of graph database implementations and what it means for them to be dependable.

CHAPTER 7

Predictive Analysis with Graph Theory

In this chapter we're going consider analytical techniques and algorithms for processing graph data. Both graph theory and graph algorithms are mature and well-understood fields of computing science and we'll demonstrate how both can can be used to mine sophisticated information from graph databases. Although the reader with a background in computing science will no doubt recognize these algorithms and techniques, the discussion in this chapter is handled without recourse to mathematics, to encourage the curious reader to dive in.

Depth- and Breadth-First Search

Before we look at higher-order analytical techniques we need to reacquaint ourselves with the fundamental *breadth-first search* algorithm, which is the basis for iterating over an entire graph. Most of the queries we've seen throughout this book have been *depth-first* rather than *breadth-first* in nature. That is, they traverse outward from a starting node to some end node before repeating a similar search down a different path from the same start node. Depth-first is a good strategy when we're trying to follow a path to discover discrete pieces of information.

Informed Depth-First Search

The classic depth-first algorithm search is *uninformed* in that it simply searches a path until it finds the end of the graph. Once at the end, it backtracks to the start node and tries a different path. Because graph databases are semantically rich, however, we can terminate a search along a particular branch early (for example, once we've found a node with no compatible outgoing relationships, or have traversed "far enough"). Such *informed* searches can result in lower execution times. These are exactly the kinds of searches performed by our Cypher matches and traversals in previous chapters.

Though we've used depth-first search as our underlying strategy for general graph traversals, many interesting "higher-order" algorithms traverse the entire graph in a *breadth-first* manner. That is, they explore the graph one layer at a time, first visiting each node at depth 1 from the start node, then each of those at depth 2, then depth 3, and so on, until the entire graph has been visited. This progression is easily visualized starting at the node labelled 0 (for *origin*) and progressing outward a layer at a time, as shown in Figure 7-1.

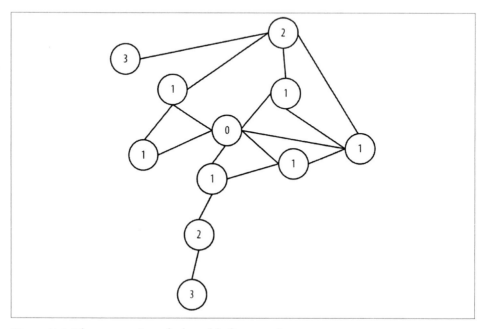

Figure 7-1. The progression of a breadth-first search

The termination of the search depends on the algorithm being executed—most useful algorithms aren't pure breadth-first search but are informed to some extent. Breadth-first search is often used in path-finding algorithms or when the entire graph needs to be systematically searched (for the likes of *graph global* algorithms we discussed in Chapter 3).

Path-Finding with Dijkstra's Algorithm

Breadth-first search underpins numerous classical graph algorithms, including Dijkstra's algorithm. Dijkstra (as it is often abbreviated) is used to find the shortest path between two nodes in a graph. Dijkstra's algorithm is mature, having been published in 1956, and thereafter widely studied and optimized by computer scientists. It behaves as follows:

1. Pick the start and end nodes, and add the start node to the set of *solved* nodes (that is, the set of nodes with known shortest path from the start node) with value 0 (the start node is by definition 0 path length away from itself).

2. From the starting node, traverse breadth-first to the nearest neighbors and record the path length against each neighbor node.

3. Take the shortest path to one of these neighbors (picking arbitrarily in the case of ties) and mark that node as solved, because we now know the shortest path from the start node to this neighbor.

4. From the set of solved nodes, visit the nearest neighbors (notice the breath-first progression) and record the path lengths from the start node against these new neighbors. Don't visit any neighboring nodes that have already been solved, because we know the shortest paths to them already.

5. Repeat steps 3 and 4 until the destination node has been marked solved.

Efficiency of Dijkstra's Algorithm

Dijkstra's algorithm is quite efficient because it computes only the lengths of a relatively small subset of the possible paths through the graph. When we've solved a node, the shortest path from the start node is then known, allowing all subsequent paths to safely build on that knowledge.

In fact, the fastest known worst-case implementation of Dijkstra's algorithm has a performance of $O(|R| + |N| \log |N|)$. That is, the algorithm runs in time proportional to the number of relationships in the graph, plus the size of the number of nodes multiplied by the log of the size of the node set. The original was $O(|R|^2)$, meaning it ran in time proportional to the square of the size of the number of relationships in the graph.

Dijkstra is often used to find real-world shortest paths (e.g., for navigation). Here's an example. In Figure 7-2 we see a logical map of Australia. Our challenge is to discover the shortest driving route between Sydney on the east coast (marked *SYD*) and Perth, marked *PER*, which is a continent away, on the west coast. The other major towns and cities are marked with their respective airport codes; we'll discover many of them along the way.

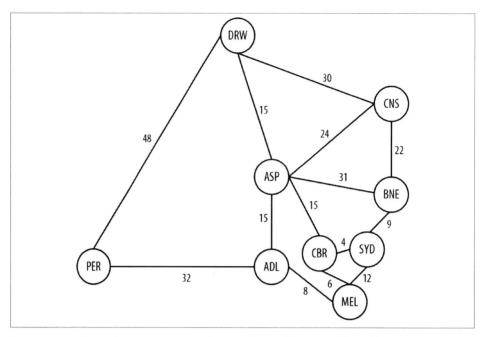

Figure 7-2. A logical representation of Australia and its arterial road network

Starting at the node representing Sydney in Figure 7-3, we know the shortest path to Sydney is 0 hours, because we're already there. In terms of Dijkstra's algorithm, Sydney is now *solved* insofar as we know the shortest path from Sydney to Sydney. Accordingly, we've grayed out the node representing Sydney, added the path length (0), and thickened the node's border—a convention that we'll maintain throughout the remainder of this example.

Moving one level out from Sydney, our candidate cities are Brisbane, which lies to the north by 9 hours, Canberra, Australia's capital city, which lies 4 hours to the west, and Melbourne, which is 12 hours to the south.

The shortest path we can find is Sydney to Canberra, at 4 hours, and so we consider Canberra to be solved, as shown in Figure 7-4.

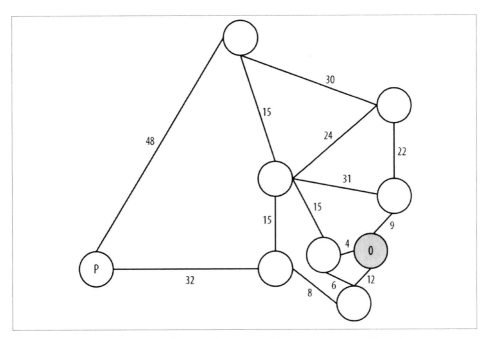

Figure 7-3. The shortest path from Sydney to Sydney is unsurprisingly 0 hours

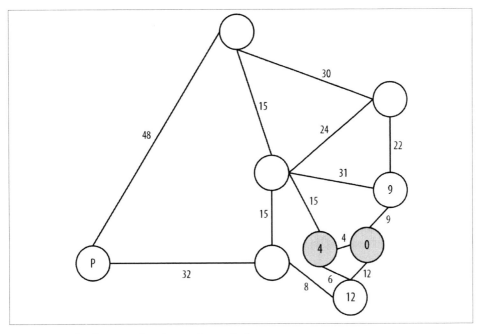

Figure 7-4. Canberra is the closest city to Sydney

The next nodes out from our solved nodes are Melbourne, at 10 hours from Sydney via Canberra, or 12 hours from Sydney directly, as we've already seen. We also have Alice Springs, which is 15 hours from Canberra and 19 hours from Sydney, or Brisbane, which is 9 hours direct from Sydney.

Accordingly, we explore the shortest path, which is 9 hours from Sydney to Brisbane, and consider Brisbane solved at 9 hours, as shown in Figure 7-5.

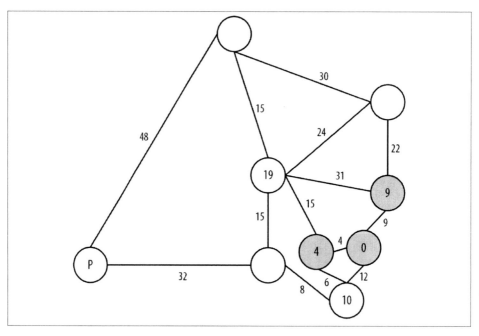

Figure 7-5. Brisbane is the next closest city

The next neighboring nodes from our solved ones are Melbourne, which is 10 hours via Canberra or 12 hours direct from Sydney along a different road; Cairns, which is 31 hours from Sydney via Brisbane; and Alice Springs, which is 40 hours via Brisbane or 19 hours via Canberra.

Accordingly, we choose the shortest path, which is Melbourne, being 10 hours from Sydney via Canberra. This is shorter than the existing 12 hours direct link. We now consider Melbourne solved, as shown in Figure 7-6.

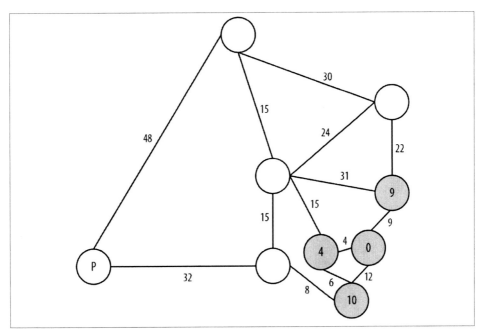

Figure 7-6. Reaching Melbourne, the third-closest city to the start node of Sydney

In Figure 7-7, the next layer of neighboring nodes from our solved ones are Adelaide at 18 hours from Sydney (via Canberra and Melbourne); Cairns, at 31 hours from Sydney (via Brisbane); and Alice Springs, at 19 hours from Sydney via Canberra, or 40 hours via Brisbane. We choose Adelaide and consider it solved at a cost of 18 hours.

 We don't consider the path Melbourne→Sydney because its destination is a solved node—in fact, in this case, it's the start node, Sydney.

The next layer of neighboring nodes from our solved ones are Perth—our final destination—which is 50 hours from Sydney via Adelaide; Alice Springs, which is 19 hours from Sydney via Canberra or 33 hours via Adelaide; and Cairns, which is 31 hours from Sydney via Brisbane.

We choose Alice Springs in this case because it has the current shortest path, even though with a god's eye view we know that actually it'll be shorter in the end to go from Adelaide to Perth—just ask any passing bushman. Our cost is 19 hours, as shown in Figure 7-8.

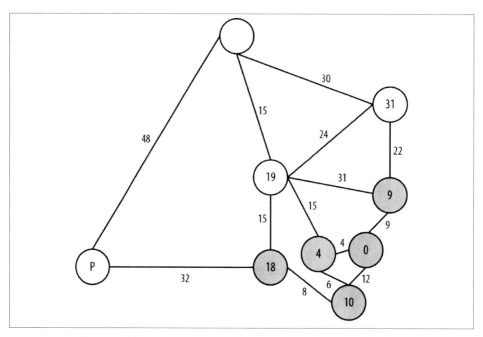

Figure 7-7. Solving Adelaide

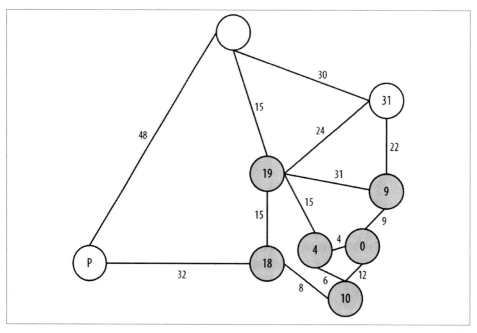

Figure 7-8. Taking a "detour" through Alice Springs

In Figure 7-9, the next layer of neighboring nodes from our solved ones are Cairns at 31 hours via Brisbane or 43 hours via Alice Springs, or Darwin at 34 hours via Alice Springs, or Perth via Adelaide at 50 hours. So we'll take the route to Cairns via Brisbane and consider Cairns solved with a shortest driving time from Sydney at 31 hours.

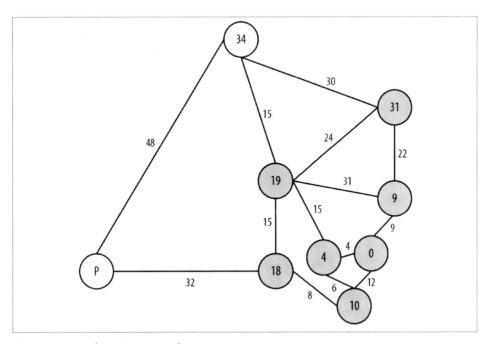

Figure 7-9. Back to Cairns on the east coast

The next layer of neighboring nodes from our solved ones are Darwin at 34 hours from Alice Springs, 61 hours via Cairns, or Perth via Adelaide at 50 hours. Accordingly, we choose the path to Darwin from Alice Springs at a cost of 34 hours and consider Darwin solved, as we can see in Figure 7-10.

Finally, the only neighboring node left is Perth itself, as we can see in Figure 7-11. It is accessible via Adelaide at a cost of 50 hours or via Darwin at a cost of 82 hours. Accordingly, we choose the route via Adelaide and consider Perth from Sydney solved at a shortest path of 50 hours.

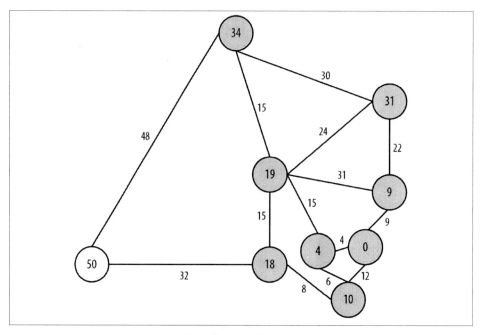

Figure 7-10. To Darwin in Australia's "top-end"

Dijkstra's algorithm works well, but because its exploration is undirected, there are some pathological graph topologies that can cause worst-case performance problems. In these situations, we explore more of the graph than is intuitively necessary, up to the entire graph. Because each possible node is considered one at a time in relative isolation, the algorithm necessarily follows paths that intuitively will never contribute to the final shortest path.

Despite Dijkstra's algorithm having successfully computed the shortest path between Sydney and Perth, anyone with any intuition about map reading would likely not have chosen to explore the route northward from Adelaide because it *feels* longer. If we had some heuristic mechanism to guide us, as in a best-first search (e.g., prefer to head west over east, prefer south over north) we might have avoided the side-trips to Brisbane, Cairns, Alice Springs, and Darwin in this example. But best-first searches are greedy, and try to move toward the destination node even if there is an obstacle (e.g., a dirt track) in the way. We can do better.

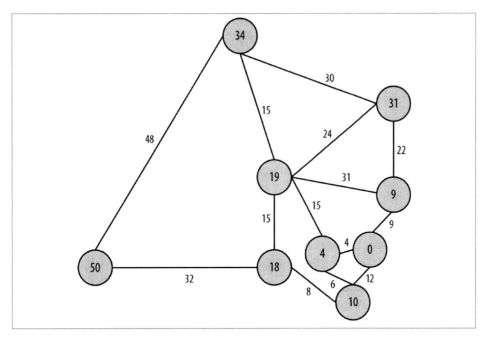

Figure 7-11. Finally reaching Perth, a mere 50 driving hours from Sydney

The A* Algorithm

The A* (pronounced "A-star") algorithm improves on the classic Dijkstra algorithm. It is based on the observation that some searches are *informed*, and that by being informed we can make better choices over which paths to take through the graph. In our example, an informed search wouldn't go from Sydney to Perth by traversing an entire continent to Darwin first. A* is both like Dijkstra in that it can potentially search a large swathe of a graph, but it's also like a greedy best-first search insofar as it uses a heuristic to guide it. A* combines aspects of Dijkstra's algorithm, which prefers nodes close to the current starting point, and best-first search, which prefers nodes closer to the destination, to provide a provably optimal solution for finding shortest paths in a graph.

In A* we split the path cost into two parts: $g(n)$, which is the cost of the path from the starting point to some node n; and $h(n)$, which represents the estimated cost of the path from the node n to the destination node, as computed by a heuristic (an intelligent guess). The A* algorithm balances $g(n)$ and $h(n)$ as it iterates the graph, thereby ensuring that at each iteration it chooses the node with the lowest overall cost $f(n) = g(n) + h(n)$.

As we've seen, breadth-first algorithms are particularly good for path finding. But they have other uses as well. Using breadth-first search as our method for iterating over all elements of a graph, we can now consider a number of interesting higher-order algorithms from graph theory that yield predictive insight into the behavior of connected data.

Graph Theory and Predictive Modeling

Graph theory is a mature and well-understood field of study concerning the nature of networks (or from our point of view, connected data). The analytic techniques that have been developed by graph theoreticians can be brought to bear on a range of interesting problems. Now that we understand the low-level traversal mechanisms, such as breadth-first search, we can start to consider higher-order analyses.

Graph theory techniques are broadly applicable to a wide range of problems. They are especially useful when we first want to gain some insight into a new domain—or even understand what kind of insight it's possible to extract from a domain. In such cases there are a range of techniques from graph theory and social sciences that we can straightforwardly apply to gain insight.

In the next few sections we'll introduce some of the key concepts in social graph theory. We'll introduce these concepts in the context of a social domain based on the works of sociologists Mark Granovetter, and Easley and Kleinberg.[1]

Property Graphs and Graph Theory

Much of the work on graph theory assumes a slightly different model to the property graphs we've been using throughout this book. This work tends to ignore direction and labeling of graphs, instead assuming undirected relationships with a single label derived from the domain (e.g., `friend` or `colleague`).

We're going to take a hybrid approach here. We'll add names to relationships where it helps add domain-specific meaning. In many cases, however, we will ignore relationship direction. This won't impact the analysis, however: the graph structure upholds the same principles irrespective of its construction.

Triadic Closures

A *triadic closure* is a common property of social graphs, where we observe that if two nodes are connected via a path involving a third node, there is an increased likelihood that the two nodes will become directly connected at some point in the future. This is a familiar social occurrence: if we happen to be friends with two people, there's an increased chance that those people will become direct friends too. The very fact of their

---

1. In particular, see Granovetter's pivotal work on the strength of weak ties in social communities: *http://stanford.io/17XjisT*. For Easley and Kleinberg, see *http://bit.ly/13e0ZuZ*.

both being our friend is an indicator that with respect to each other they may be socially similar.

From his analysis, Granovetter noted that a subgraph upholds the *strong triadic closure property* if it has a node *A* with strong relationships to two other nodes, *B* and *C*. *B* and *C* then have at least a *weak*, and potentially a *strong*, relationship between them. This is a bold assertion, and it won't always hold for all subgraphs in a graph. Nonetheless, it is sufficiently commonplace, particularly in social networks, as to be a credible predictive indicator.

Strong and Weak Relationships

We're not going to define *weak* and *strong* relationships, because they're specific to each domain. In a social communications network, a strong social relationship might be said to exist between friends who've exchanged phone calls in the last week, whereas a weak social relationship might be said to connect friends who've merely observed one-another's Facebook status.

Let's see how the strong triadic closure property works as a predictive aid in a workplace graph. We'll start with a simple organizational hierarchy in which Alice manages Bob and Charlie, but where there are not yet any connections between her subordinates, as shown in Figure 7-12.

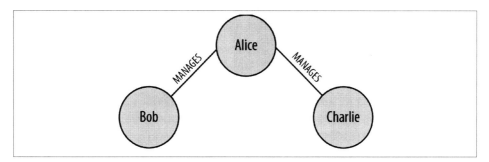

Figure 7-12. Alice manages Bob and Charlie

This is a rather strange situation for the workplace. After all, it's unlikely that Bob and Charlie will be total strangers to one another. As shown in Figure 7-13, whether they're high-level executives and therefore peers under Alice's executive management or whether they're assembly-line workers and therefore close colleagues under Alice acting as foreman, even informally we might expect Bob and Charlie to be somehow connected.

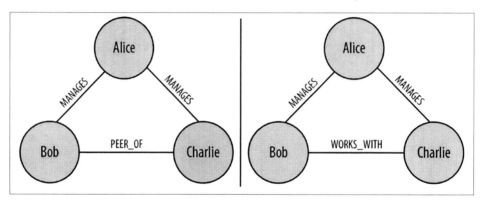

Figure 7-13. Bob and Charlie work together under Alice

Because Bob and Charlie both work with Alice, there's a strong possibility they're going to end up working together, as we see in Figure 7-13. This is consistent with the strong triadic closure property, which suggests that either Bob is a peer of Charlie (we'll call this a *weak* relationship) or that Bob works with Charlie (which we'll term a *strong* relationship). Adding a third WORKS_WITH or PEER_OF relationship between Bob and Charlie closes the triangle—hence the term *triadic closure*.

The empirical evidence from many domains, including sociology, public health, psychology, anthropology, and even technology (e.g., Facebook, Twitter, LinkedIn), suggests that the tendency toward triadic closure is real and substantial. This is consistent with anecdotal evidence and sentiment. But simple geometry isn't all that's at work here: the quality of the relationships involved in a graph also have a significant bearing on the formation of *stable* triadic closures.

Structural Balance

If we recall Figure 7-12 it's intuitive to see how Bob and Charlie can become coworkers (or peers) under Alice's management. For example purposes, we're going to make an assumption that the MANAGES relationship is somewhat negative (after all, people don't like getting bossed around) whereas the PEER_OF and WORKS_WITH relationship are positive (because people like their peers and the folks they work with).

We know from our previous discussion on the strong triadic closure principle that in Figure 7-12 where Alice MANAGES Bob and Charlie, a triadic closure should be formed. That is, in the absence of any other constraints, we would expect at least a PEER_OF, a WORKS_WITH, or even a MANAGES relationship between Bob and Charlie.

A similar tendency toward creating a triadic closure exists if Alice MANAGES Bob who in turn WORKS_WITH Charlie, as we can see in Figure 7-14. Anecdotally this rings true: if Bob and Charlie work together it makes sense for them to share a manager, especially if the organization seemingly allows Charlie to function without managerial supervision.

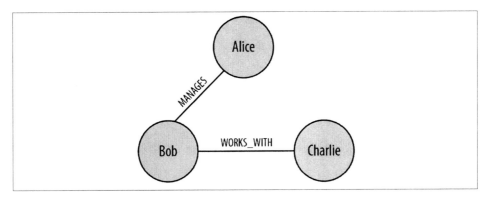

Figure 7-14. Alice manages Bob who works with Charlie

However, applying the strong triadic closure principle blindly can lead to some rather odd and uncomfortable-looking organization hierarchies. For instance, if Alice MAN AGES Bob and Charlie but Bob also MANAGES Charlie, we have a recipe for discontent. Nobody would wish it upon Charlie that he's managed both by his boss and his boss's boss as in Figure 7-15!

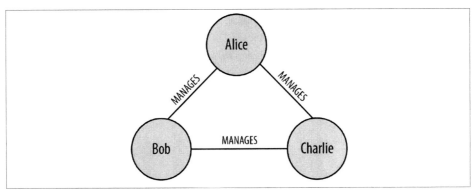

Figure 7-15. Alice manages Bob and Charlie, while Bob also manages Charlie

Similarly, it's uncomfortable for Bob if he is managed by Alice while working with Charlie who is also Alice's workmate. This cuts awkwardly across organization layers as we see in Figure 7-16. It also means Bob could never safely let off steam about Alice's management style!

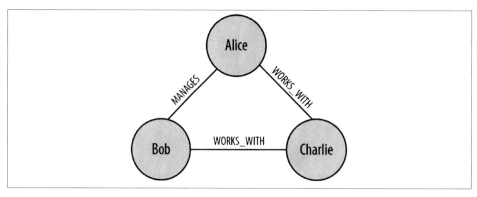

Figure 7-16. Alice manages Bob who works with Charlie, while also working with Charlie

The awkward hierarchy in Figure 7-16 whereby Charlie is both a peer of the boss and a peer of another worker is unlikely to be socially pleasant, so Charlie and Alice will agitate against it (either wanting to be a boss or a worker). It's similar for Bob who doesn't know for sure whether to treat Charlie in the same way he treats his manager Alice (because Charlie and Alice are peers) or as his own direct peer.

It's clear that the triadic closures in Figure 7-15 and Figure 7-16 are palpably uncomfortable to us, eschewing our innate preference for structural symmetry and rational layering. This preference is given a name in graph theory: *structural balance*.

Anecdotally, there's a much more acceptable, structurally balanced triadic closure if Alice MANAGES Bob and Charlie, but where Bob and Charlie are themselves workmates connected by a WORKS_WITH relationship, as we can see in Figure 7-17.

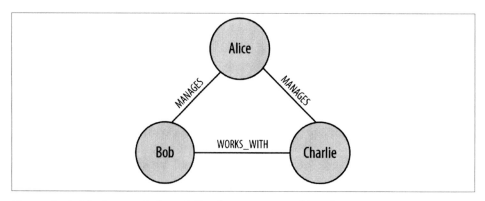

Figure 7-17. Workmates Bob and Charlie are managed by Alice

The same structural balance manifests itself in an equally acceptable triadic closure where Alice, Bob, and Charlie are all workmates. In this arrangement the workers are in it together, which can be a socially amicable arrangement that engenders camaraderie as in Figure 7-18.

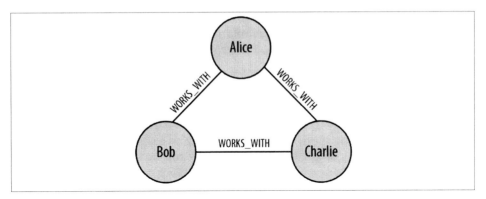

Figure 7-18. Alice, Bob, and Charlie are all workmates

In Figure 7-17 and Figure 7-18 the triadic closures are idiomatic and constructed with either three WORKS_WITH relationships or two MANAGES and a single WORKS_WITH relationship. They are all *balanced* triadic closures. To understand what it means to have balanced and unbalanced triadic closures, we'll add more semantic richness to the model by declaring that the WORKS_WITH relationship is socially positive (because coworkers spend a lot of time interacting), whereas MANAGES is a negative relationship because managers spend overall less of their time interacting with individuals in their charge.

Given this new dimension of positive and negative sentiment, we can now ask the question "What is so special about these balanced structures?" It's clear that strong triadic closure is still at work, but that's not the only driver. In this case the notion of *structural balance* also has an effect. A structurally balanced triadic closure consists of relationships of all strong sentiments (our WORKS_WITH or PEER_OF relationships) or two relationships have negative sentiments (MANAGES in our case) with a single positive relationship.

We see this often in the real world. If we have two good friends, then social pressure tends toward those good friends themselves becoming good friends. It's unusual that those two friends themselves are enemies because that puts a strain on our friendships. One friend cannot express his dislike of the other to us, because the other person is our friend too! Given those pressures, it's reasonably likely that ultimately the group will resolve its differences and good friends will emerge.

This would change our unbalanced triadic closure (two relationships with positive sentiments and one negative) to a balanced closure because all relationships would be of a positive sentiment much like our collaborative scheme where Alice, Bob, and Charlie all work together in Figure 7-18.

However, another plausible (though arguably less pleasant) outcome would be where we take sides in the dispute between our "friends" creating two relationships with negative sentiments—effectively ganging up on an individual. Now we can engage in gossip about our mutual dislike of a former friend and the closure again becomes balanced. Equally we see this reflected in the organizational scenario where Alice, by managing Bob and Charlie, becomes, in effect, their workplace enemy as in Figure 7-17.

Mining Organizational Data in the Real World

We don't have to derive these graphs from analyzing organizational charts, because that's a static and often inconsistent view of how an organization really works. A practical and timely way of generating the graph would instead be to run these kinds of analyses over the history of email exchanges between individuals within a company.

We'd easily be able to identify a graph at large scale and from that we'd be able to make predictive analyses about the evolution of organizational structure by looking for opportunities to create balanced closures. Such structures might be a boon—that we observe employees are already self-organizing for a successful outcome; or they might be indicative of some malpractice—that some employees are moving into shadowy corners to commit corporate fraud! Either way, the predictive power of graphs enables us to engage those issues proactively.

Balanced closures add another dimension to the predictive power of graphs. Simply by looking for opportunities to create balanced closures across a graph, even at very large scale, we can modify the graph structure for accurate predictive analyses. But we can go further, and in the next section we'll bring in the notion of *local bridges*, which give us valuable insight into the communications flow of our organization, and from that knowledge comes the ability to adapt it to meet future challenges.

Local Bridges

An organization of only three people as we've been using is anomalous, and the graphs we've studied in this section are best thought of as small subgraphs as part of a larger organizational hierarchy. When we start to consider managing a larger organization we expect a much more complex graph structure, but we can also apply other heuristics to the structure to help make sense of the business. In fact, once we have introduced other parts of the organization into the graph, we can reason about global properties of the graph based on the locally acting strong triadic closure principle.

In Figure 7-19 we're presented with a counterintuitive scenario where two groups in the organization are managed by Alice and Davina, respectively. However, we have the slightly awkward structure that Alice not only runs a team with Bob and Charlie, but also manages Davina. Though this isn't beyond the realm of possibility (Alice may indeed have such responsibilities), it feels intuitively awkward from an organization design perspective.

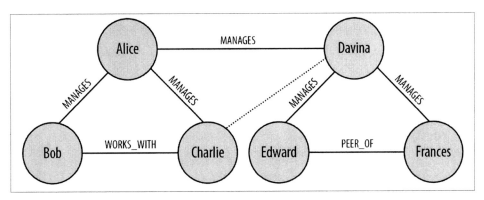

Figure 7-19. Alice has skewed line management responsibility

From a graph theory perspective it's also unlikely. Because Alice participates in two strong relationships, she MANAGES Charlie (and Bob) and MANAGES Davina, naturally we'd like to create a triadic closure by adding at least a PEER_OF relationship between Davina and Charlie (and Bob). But Alice is also involved in a *local bridge* to Davina—together they're a sole communication path between groups in the organization. Having the relationship Alice MANAGES Davina means we'd in fact have to create the closure. These two properties—local bridge and strong triadic closure—are in opposition.

Yet if Alice and Davina are peers (a weak relationship), then the strong triadic closure principle isn't activated because there's only one strong relationship—the MANAGES relationship to Bob (or Charlie)—and the local bridge property is valid as we can see in Figure 7-20.

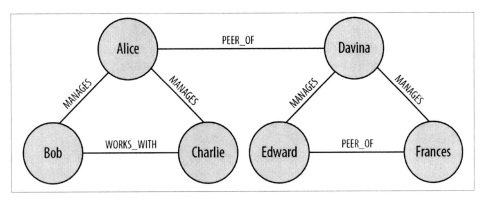

Figure 7-20. Alice and Davina are connected by a local bridge

What's interesting about this local bridge is that it describes a communication channel between groups in our organization. Such channels are extremely important to the vitality of our enterprise. In particular, to ensure the health of our company we'd make sure that local bridge relationships are healthy and active, or equally we might keep an eye on local bridges to ensure no impropriety (embezzlement, fraud, etc.) occurs.

Finding Your Next Job

This notion of weak social links is particularly pertinent in algorithms like (social) job search. The remarkable thing about job searches is that it's rarely a close friend that provides the best recommendation, but a looser acquaintance.

Why should this be? Our close friends share a similar world view (they're in the same *graph component*) and have similar access to the available jobs data and hold similar opinions about those jobs. A friend across a local bridge is clearly in a different social network (a different component), with correspondingly different access to jobs and a different viewpoint about them. So if you're going to find a job, look across a local bridge because that's where people who have different knowledge to you and your friends hang out.

This same property of local bridges being weak links (PEER_OF in our example organization) is a property that is prevalent throughout social graphs. This means we can start to make predictive analyses of how our organization will evolve based on empirically derived local bridge and strong triadic closure notions. So given an arbitrary organizational graph, we can see how the business structure is likely to evolve and plan for those eventualities.

Summary

Graphs are truly remarkable structures. Our understanding of them is rooted in several hundred years of mathematical and scientific study. And yet we're only just beginning to understand how to apply them to our personal, social, and business lives. The technology is here, open and available to all in the form of the modern graph database; the opportunities are endless.

As we've seen throughout this book, graph theory algorithms and analytical techniques are not demanding: we need only understand how to *apply* them to achieve our goals. We leave this book with a simple call to arms: embrace graphs and graph databases; take all that you've learned about modeling with graphs, graph database architecture, designing and implementing a graph database solution, and applying graph algorithms to complex business problems, and go build the next truly pioneering information system.

NOSQL Overview

Recent years have seen a meteoric rise in popularity of a family of data storage technologies known as *NOSQL* (a cheeky acronym for *Not Only SQL*, or more confrontationally, *No to SQL*). But NOSQL as a term defines what those data stores are not—they're not SQL-centric relational databases—rather than what they are, which is an interesting and useful set of storage technologies whose operational, functional, and architectural characteristics are many and varied.

Why were these new databases created? What problems do they address? Here we'll discuss some of the new data challenges that have emerged in the past decade. We'll then look at four families of NOSQL databases, including graph databases.

The Rise of NOSQL

Historically, most enterprise-level web apps ran on top of a relational database. But in the past decade, we've been faced with data that is bigger in volume, changes more rapidly, and is more structurally varied than can be dealt with by traditional RDBMS deployments. The NOSQL movement has arisen in response to these challenges.

It's no surprise that as storage has increased dramatically, *volume* has become the principal driver behind the adoption of NOSQL stores by organizations. Volume may be defined simply as *the size of the stored data*.

As is well known, large datasets become unwieldy when stored in relational databases; in particular, query execution times increase as the size of tables and the number of joins grow (so-called *join pain*). This isn't the fault of the databases themselves; rather, it is an aspect of the underlying data model, which builds a set of all possible answers to a query before filtering to arrive at the correct solution.

In an effort to avoid joins and join pain, and thereby cope better with extremely large datasets, the NOSQL world has adopted several alternatives to the relational model.

Though more adept at dealing with very large datasets, these alternative models tend to be less expressive than the relational one (with the exception of the graph model, which is actually *more* expressive).

But volume isn't the only problem modern web-facing systems have to deal with. Besides being big, today's data often changes very rapidly. *Velocity* is the rate at which data changes over time.

Velocity is rarely a static metric: internal and external changes to a system and the context in which it is employed can have considerable impact on velocity. Coupled with high volume, variable velocity requires data stores to not only handle sustained levels of high write loads, but also deal with peaks.

There is another aspect to velocity, which is the rate at which the structure of the data changes. In other words, in addition to the value of specific properties changing, the overall structure of the elements hosting those properties can change as well. This commonly occurs for two reasons. The first is fast-moving business dynamics: as the business changes, so do its data needs. The second is that data acquisition is often an experimental affair: some properties are captured "just in case," others are introduced at a later point based on changed needs; the ones that prove valuable to the business stay around, others fall by the wayside. Both these forms of velocity are problematic in the relational world, where high write loads translate into a high processing cost, and high schema volatility has a high operational cost.

Although commentators have later added other useful requirements to the original quest for scale, the final key aspect is the realization that data is far more varied than the data we've dealt with in the relational world. For existential proof, think of all those nulls in our tables and the null checks in our code. This has driven out the final widely agreed upon facet, *variety*, which we define as the degree to which data is regularly or irregularly structured, dense or sparse, connected or disconnected.

ACID versus BASE

When we first encounter NOSQL we often consider it in the context of what many of us are already familiar with: relational databases. Although we know the data and query model will be different (after all, there's no SQL!), the consistency models used by NOSQL stores can also be quite different from those employed by relational databases. Many NOSQL databases use different consistency models to support the differences in volume, velocity, and variety of data discussed earlier.

Let's explore what consistency features are available to help keep data safe, and what trade-offs are involved when using (most) NOSQL stores.[1]

In the relational database world, we're all familiar with *ACID* transactions, which have been the norm for some time. The ACID guarantees provide us with a safe environment in which to operate on data:

Atomic
All operations in a transaction succeed or every operation is rolled back.

Consistent
On transaction completion, the database is structurally sound.

Isolated
Transactions do not contend with one another. Contentious access to state is moderated by the database so that transactions appear to run sequentially.

Durable
The results of applying a transaction are permanent, even in the presence of failures.

These properties mean that once a transaction completes, its data is consistent (so-called *write consistency*) and stable on disk (or disks, or indeed in multiple distinct memory locations). This is a wonderful abstraction for the application developer, but requires sophisticated locking, which can cause logical unavailability, and is typically considered to be a heavyweight pattern for most use cases.

For many domains, ACID transactions are far more pessimistic than the domain actually requires. In the NOSQL world, ACID transactions have gone out of fashion as stores loosen the requirements for immediate consistency, data freshness, and accuracy in order to gain other benefits, like scale and resilience. Instead of using ACID, the term *BASE* has arisen as a popular way of describing the properties of a more optimistic storage strategy.

Basic availability
The store appears to work most of the time.

Soft-state
Stores don't have to be write-consistent, nor do different replicas have to be mutually consistent all the time.

Eventual consistency
Stores exhibit consistency at some later point (e.g., lazily at read time).

The BASE properties are considerably looser than the ACID guarantees, and there is no direct mapping between them. A BASE store values availability (because that is a

---

1. The .NET-based RavenDB has bucked the trend among aggregate stores in supporting ACID transactions; as we show elsewhere in the book, ACID properties are still upheld by many graph databases.

core building block for scale), but does not offer guaranteed consistency of replicas at write time. BASE stores provide a less strict assurance: that data will be consistent in the future, perhaps at read time (e.g., Riak), or will always be consistent, but only for certain processed past snapshots (e.g., Datomic).

Given such loose support for consistency, we as developers need to be more knowledgable and rigorous when considering data consistency. We must be familiar with the BASE behavior of our chosen stores and work within those constraints. At the application level we must choose on a case-by-case basis whether we will accept potentially inconsistent data, or whether we will instruct the database to provide consistent data at read time, incurring the latency penalty that that implies. (In order to guarantee consistent reads, the database will need to compare all replicas of a data element, and in an inconsistent outcome even perform remedial repair work on that data.) From a development perspective this is a far cry from the simplicity of relying on transactions to manage consistent state on our behalf, and though that's not necessarily a bad thing, it does require effort.

The NOSQL Quadrants

Having discussed the BASE model that underpins consistency in NOSQL stores, we're ready to start looking at the numerous user-level data models. To disambiguate these models, we've devised a simple taxonomy, as shown in Figure A-1. This taxonomy divides the contemporary NOSQL space into four quadrants. Stores in each quadrant address a different kind of functional use case—though nonfunctional requirements can also strongly influence our choice of database.

In the following sections we'll deal with each of these quadrants, highlighting the characteristics of the data model, operational aspects, and drivers for adoption.

Document Stores

Document databases offer the most immediately familiar paradigm for developers who are used to working with hierarchically structured documents. Document databases store and retrieve documents, just like an electronic filing cabinet. Documents tend to comprise maps and lists, allowing for natural hierarchies—much as we're used to with formats like JSON and XML.

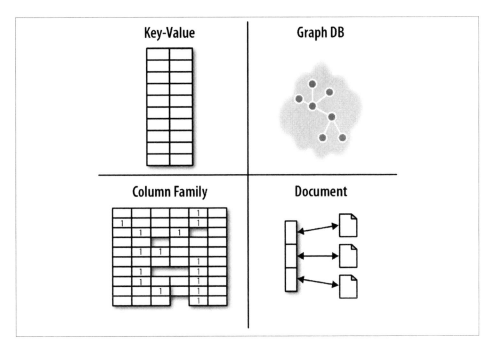

Figure A-1. The NOSQL store quadrants

At the simplest level, documents can be stored and retrieved by ID. Providing an application remembers the IDs it's interested in (e.g., usernames), a document store can act much like a key-value store (of which we'll see more later). But in the general case, document stores rely on indexes to facilitate access to documents based on their attributes. For example, in an ecommerce scenario, we might use indexes to represent distinct product types so that they can be offered up to potential sellers, as shown in Figure A-2. In general, indexes are used to retrieve sets of related documents from the store for an application to use.

Much like indexes in relational databases, indexes in a document store enable us to trade write performance for greater read performance; that is, writes are more costly, because they also maintain indexes, but reads require scanning fewer records to find pertinent data. For write-heavy records, it's worth bearing in mind that indexes might actually degrade performance overall.

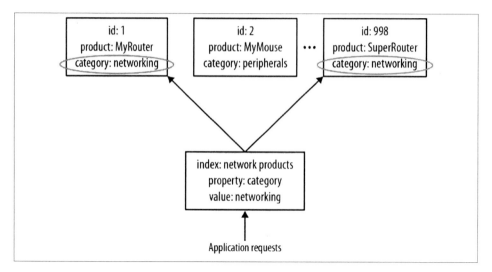

Figure A-2. Indexing reifies sets of entities in a document store

Where data hasn't been indexed, queries are typically much slower, because a full search of the dataset has to happen. This is obviously an expensive task and is to be avoided wherever possible—and as we shall see, rather than process these queries internally, it's normal for document database users to externalize this kind of processing in parallel compute frameworks.

Because the data model of a document store is one of disconnected entities, document stores tend to have interesting and useful operational characteristics. They *should* scale horizontally, due to there being no contended state between mutually independent records at write time, and no need to transact across replicas.

Sharding

Most document databases (e.g., MongoDB, RavenDB) require users to plan for *sharding* of data across logical instances to support scaling horizontally. Scaling out thus becomes an explicit aspect of development and operations. (Key-value and column family databases, in contrast, tend not to require this planning, because they allocate data to replicas as a normal part of their internal implementation.) This is sometimes puzzlingly cited as a positive reason for choosing document stores, most likely because it induces a (misplaced) excitement that scale is something to be embraced and lauded, rather than something to be skillfully and diligently mastered.

For writes, document databases tend to provide transactionality limited to the level of an individual record. That is, a document database will ensure that writes to a single document are atomically persisted—assuming the administrator has opted for safe

---

levels of persistence when setting up the database. There is no locking support, however, for operating across sets of documents atomically. Such abstractions are left to application code to implement in a domain-specific manner.

Because stored documents are not connected (save through indexes), there are numerous optimistic concurrency control mechanisms that can be used to help reconcile concurrent contending writes for a single document without having to resort to strict locks. In fact, some document stores (like CouchDB) have made this a key point of their value proposition: documents can be held in a multimaster database that automatically replicates concurrently accessed, contended state across instances without undue interference from the user.

In other stores, too, the database management system may be able to distinguish and reconcile writes to different parts of a document, or even use logical timestamps to reconcile several contended writes into a single logically consistent outcome. This is a reasonable optimistic trade-off: it reduces the need for transactions (which we know tend to be latent and decrease availability) by using alternative mechanisms that optimistically provide greater availability, lower latency, and higher throughput.

 Though optimistic concurrency control mechanisms are useful, we also rather like transactions, and there are numerous examples of high-throughput performance transaction processing systems in the literature.

Key-Value Stores

Key-value stores are cousins of the document store family, but their lineage comes from Amazon's Dynamo database (*http://www.allthingsdistributed.com/files/amazon-dynamo-sosp2007.pdf*). They act like large, distributed hashmap data structures that store and retrieve opaque values by key.

As shown in Figure A-3 the key space of the hashmap is spread across numerous buckets on the network. For fault-tolerance reasons, each bucket is replicated onto several machines. The formula for number of replicas required is given by $R = 2F + 1$, where F is the number of failures we can tolerate. The replication algorithm seeks to ensure that machines aren't exact copies of each other. This allows the system to load-balance while a machine and its buckets recover; it also helps avoid hotspots, which can cause inadvertent self denial-of-service.

From the client's point of view, key-value stores are easy to use. A client stores a data element by hashing a domain-specific identifier (key). The hash function is crafted such that it provides a uniform distribution across the available buckets, which ensures that no single machine becomes a hotspot. Given the hashed key, the client can use that address to store the value in a corresponding bucket. Clients use a similar process to retrieve stored values.

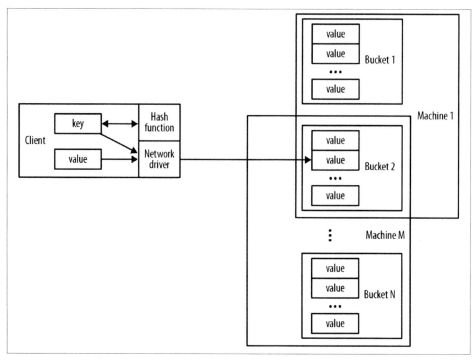

Figure A-3. Key-value stores act like distributed hashmap data structures

Consistent Hashing

Failures will occur in all computer systems. In dependable systems those failures are masked via redundant replacements being switched in for faulty components. In a key-value store—as with any distributed database—individual machines will likely become unavailable during normal operation as networks go down, or as hardware fails. Such events are considered normal, so long as the side effects of recovering from such failures don't cause further problems. For example, if a machine supporting a particular hash-range fails, it should not prevent new values in that range being stored or cause unavailability while internal reorganization occurs.

This is where *consistent hashing* (*http://en.wikipedia.org/wiki/Consistent_hashing*) comes into play. With this technique, writes to a failed hash-range are cheaply remapped to the next available machine without disturbing the entire stored dataset. In fact, in many cases, only a fraction of the keys within the failed range need to be remapped, rather than the whole set. When the failed machine recovers or is replaced, consistent hashing again ensures only a fraction of the total key space is remapped.

Given such a model, applications wishing to store data in, or retrieve data from, a key-value store need only know (or compute) the corresponding key. Although there is a very large number of possible keys in the key set, in practice keys tend to fall out quite naturally from the application domain. Usernames and email addresses, Cartesian coordinates for places of interest, Social Security numbers, and zip codes are all natural keys for various domains. With a sensibly designed system, the chance of losing data in the store due to a missing key is low.

The key-value data model is similar to the document data model. What differentiates them is the level of *insight* each offers into its data.

In theory, key-value stores are oblivious to the information contained in their values. Pure key-value stores simply concern themselves with efficient storage and retrieval of opaque data on behalf of applications, unencumbered by its nature and application usage.

Opacity and Access to Subelements Inside Structured Data

Opacity has a downside. When extracting an element of data from a stored value, clients often have to retrieve the whole value, and then filter out the unwanted parent or sibling data elements. Compared to document stores, which perform such operations on the server, this can be somewhat inefficient.

In practice, such distinctions aren't always so clear-cut. Some of the popular key-value stores—Riak, for instance—also offer visibility into certain types of structured stored data like XML and JSON. At a product level, then, there is some overlap between the document and key-value stores.

Although simple, the key-value model, much as the document model, offers little in the way of data insight to the application developer. To retrieve sets of useful information from across individual records, we typically use an external processing infrastructure, such as MapReduce. This is highly latent compared to executing queries in the data store.

Key-value stores offer certain operational and scale advantages. Descended as they are from Amazon's Dynamo database—a platform designed for a nonstop shopping cart service—they tend to be optimized for high availability and scale. Or, as the Amazon team puts it, they should work even "if disks are failing, network routes are flapping, or data centers are being destroyed by tornados."

Column Family

Column family stores are modeled on Google's BigTable (*http://research.google.com/archive/bigtable.html*). The data model is based on a sparsely populated table whose rows can contain arbitrary columns, the keys for which provide natural indexing.

 In our discussion we'll use terminology from Apache Cassandra. Cassandra isn't necessarily a faithful interpretation of BigTable, but it is widely deployed, and its terminology is well understood.

In Figure A-4 we see the four common building blocks used in column family databases. The simplest unit of storage is the *column* itself, consisting of a name-value pair. Any number of columns can be combined into a *super column*, which gives a name to a sorted set of columns. Columns are stored in rows, and when a row contains columns only, it is known as a *column family*. When a row contains super columns, it is known as a *super column family*.

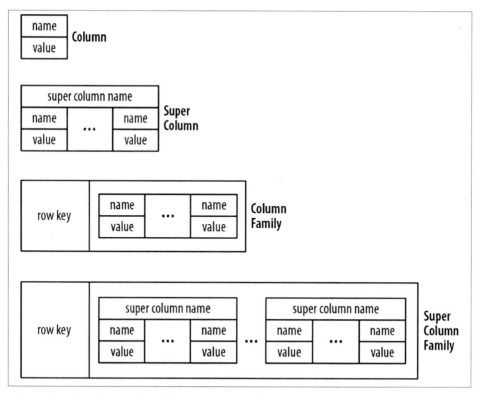

Figure A-4. The four building blocks of column family storage

It might seem odd to focus on rows when the data model is ostensibly columnar, but individual level rows really are important, because they provide the nested hashmap structure into which we decompose our data. In Figure A-5 we show how we might map a recording artist and his albums into a super column family structure—logically, it's really nothing more than maps of maps.

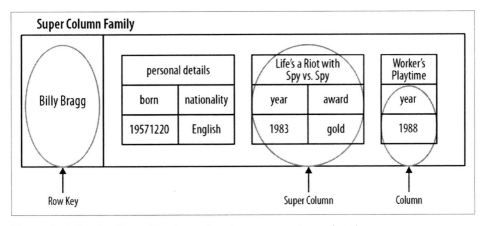

Figure A-5. *Storing line-of-business data in a super column family*

In a column family database, each row in the table represents a particular overarching entity (e.g., everything about an artist). These column families are containers for related pieces of data, such as the artist's name and discography. Within the column families we find actual key-value data, such as album release dates and the artist's date of birth.

Helpfully, this row-oriented view can be turned through 90 degrees to arrive at a column-oriented view. Where each row gives a complete view of one entity, the column view naturally indexes particular aspects across the whole dataset. For example, as we see in Figure A-6, by "lining up" keys we are able to find all the rows where the artist is English. From there it's easy to extract complete artist data from each row. It's not connected data as we'd find in a graph, but it does at least provide some insight into a set of related entities.

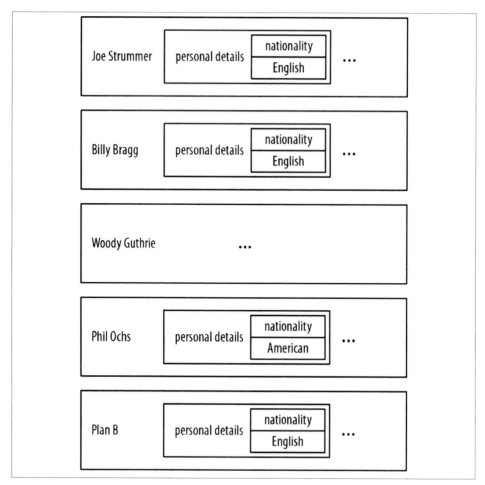

Figure A-6. Keys form a natural index through rows in a column family database

Column family databases are distinguished from document and key-value stores not only by their more expressive data model, but also by their operational characteristics. Apache Cassandra, for example, which is based on a Dynamo-like infrastructure, is architected for distribution, scale, and failover. Under the covers it uses several storage engines that deal with high write loads—the kind of peak write loads generated by popular interactive TV shows.

Overall, column family databases are reasonably expressive and operationally very competent. And yet they're still *aggregate stores*, just like document and key-value databases, and as such, lack joins. Querying them for insight into data at scale requires processing by some external application infrastructure.

Query versus Processing in Aggregate Stores

In the preceding sections we've highlighted the similarities and differences between the document, key-value, and column family data models. On balance, the similarities have been greater than the differences. In fact, the similarities are so great, the three types are sometimes referred to jointly as *aggregate stores* (*http://martinfowler.com/bliki/Nosql Distilled.html*). Aggregate stores persist standalone complex records that reflect the Domain-Driven Design notion (*http://domaindrivendesign.org/*) of an *aggregate*.

Each aggregate store has a different storage strategy, yet they all have a great deal in common when it comes to querying data. For simple ad hoc queries, each tends to provide features such as indexing, simple document linking, or a query language. For more complex queries, applications commonly identify and extract a subset of data from the store before piping it through some external processing infrastructure such as a MapReduce framework. This is done when the necessary deep insight cannot be generated simply by examining individual aggregates.

MapReduce (*http://research.google.com/archive/mapreduce.html*), like BigTable, is another technique that comes to us from Google. The most prevalent open source implementations of MapReduce is Apache Hadoop and its attendant ecosystem.

MapReduce is a parallel programming model that splits data and operates on it in parallel before gathering it back together and aggregating it to provide focused information. If, for example, we wanted to use it to count how many American artists there are in a recording artists database, we'd extract all the artist records and discard the non-American ones in the map phase, and then count the remaining records in the reduce phase.

Even with a lot of machines and a fast network infrastructure, MapReduce can be quite latent. Normally, we'd use the features of the data store to provide a more focused dataset —perhaps using indexes or other ad hoc queries—and then MapReduce that smaller dataset to arrive at our answer.

Aggregate stores are not built to deal with highly connected data. We can use them for that purpose, but we have to add code to fill in where the underlying data model leaves off, resulting in a development experience that is far from seamless, and operational characteristics that are generally speaking not very fast, particularly as the number of hops (or "degree" of the query) increases. Aggregate stores may be good at strong data that's big, but they aren't generally that great at dealing with problems that require an understanding of how things are connected.

Graph Databases

A *graph database* is an online ("real-time") database management system with Create, Read, Update, and Delete (CRUD) methods that expose a graph data model. Graph databases are generally built for use with transactional (OLTP) systems. Accordingly, they are normally optimized for transactional performance, and engineered with transactional integrity and operational availability in mind.

Two properties of graph databases are useful to understand when investigating graph database technologies:

The underlying storage

> Some graph databases use *native graph storage*, which is optimized and designed for storing and managing graphs. Not all graph database technologies use native graph storage, however. Some serialize the graph data into a relational database, object-oriented databases, or other types of general-purpose data stores.

The processing engine

> Some definitions of graph databases require that they be capable of *index-free adjacency*,[2] meaning that connected nodes physically "point" to each other in the database. Here we take a slightly broader view: that any database that from the user's perspective behaves like a graph database (i.e., exposes a graph data model through CRUD operations), qualifies as a graph database. We do acknowledge, however, the significant performance advantages of index-free adjacency, and therefore use the term *native graph processing* in reference to graph databases that leverage index-free adjacency.

Graph databases—in particular native ones—don't depend heavily on indexes because the graph itself provides a natural adjacency index. In a native graph database, the relationships attached to a node naturally provide a direct connection to other related nodes of interest. Graph queries largely involve using this locality to traverse through the graph, literally chasing pointers. These operations can be carried out with extreme efficiency, traversing millions of nodes per second, in contrast to joining data through a global index, which is many orders of magnitude slower.

There are several different graph data models, including property graphs, hypergraphs, and triples.

Property Graphs

A property graph has the following characteristics:

- It contains nodes and relationships
- Nodes contain properties (key-value pairs)
- Relationships are named and directed, and always have a start and end node

---

2. See Rodriguez, M.A., Neubauer, P., "The Graph Traversal Pattern," 2010 (*http://arxiv.org/abs/1004.1001*).

- Relationships can also contain properties

Hypergraphs

A hypergraph is a generalized graph model in which a relationship (called a hyper-edge) can connect any number of nodes. Whereas the property graph model permits a relationship to have only one start node and one end node, the hypergraph model allows any number of nodes at either end of a relationship. Hypergraphs can be useful where the domain consists mainly of many-to-many relationships. For example, in Figure A-7 we see that Alice and Bob are the owners of three vehicles. We express this using a single hyper-edge, whereas in a property graph we would use six relationships.

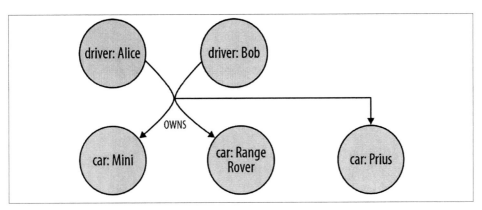

Figure A-7. A simple (directed) hypergraph

As we discussed in Chapter 3, graphs enable us to model our problem domain in a way that is easy to visualize and understand, and which captures with high fidelity the many nuances of the data we encounter in the real world. Although in theory hypergraphs produce accurate, information-rich models, in practice it's very easy for us to miss some detail while modeling. To illustrate this point, let's consider the graph shown in Figure A-8, which is the property graph equivalent of the hypergraph shown in Figure A-7.

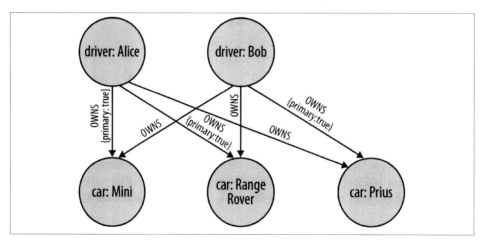

Figure A-8. A property graph is semantically fine-tuned

The property graph shown here requires several OWNS relationships to express what the hypergraph captured with just one. But in using several relationships, not only are we able to use a familiar and very explicit modeling technique, but we're also able to fine-tune the model. For example, we've identified the "primary driver" for each vehicle (for insurance purposes) by adding a property to the relevant relationships—something that can't be done with a single hyper-edge.

> Because hyper-edges are multidimensional, hypergraphs comprise a more general model than property graphs. That said, the two models are isomorphic; it is always possible to represent the information in a hypergraph as a property graph (albeit using more relationships and intermediary nodes). Whether a hypergraph or a property graph is best for you is going to depend on your modeling mindset and the kinds of applications you're building. Anecdotally, for most purposes property graphs are widely considered to have the best balance of pragmatism and modeling efficiency—hence their overwhelming popularity in the graph database space. However, in situations where you need to capture meta-intent, effectively qualifying one relationship with another (e.g., I like the fact that you liked that car), hypergraphs typically require fewer primitives than property graphs.

Triples

Triple stores come from the Semantic Web movement, where researchers are interested in large-scale knowledge inference by adding semantic markup to the links that connect web resources (*http://www.w3.org/standards/semanticweb/*). To date, very little of the Web has been marked up in a useful fashion, so running queries across the semantic layer is uncommon. Instead, most effort in the Semantic Web appears to be invested in harvesting useful data and relationship information from the Web (or other more mundane data sources, such as applications) and depositing it in *triple stores* for querying.

A triple is a *subject-predicate-object* data structure. Using triples, we can capture facts, such as "Ginger dances with Fred" and "Fred likes ice cream." Individually, single triples are semantically rather poor, but en-masse they provide a rich dataset from which to harvest knowledge and *infer* connections. Triple stores typically provide SPARQL capabilities (*http://www.w3.org/TR/rdf-sparql-query/*) to reason about and stored RDF data (*http://www.w3.org/RDF/*).

RDF—the lingua franca of triple stores and the Semantic Web—can be serialized several ways. The following snippet shows how triples come together to form linked data, using the RDF/XML format:

```
<rdf:RDF xmlns:rdf="http://www.w3.org/1999/02/22-rdf-syntax-ns#"
         xmlns="http://www.example.org/terms/">
    <rdf:Description rdf:about="http://www.example.org/ginger">
        <name>Ginger Rogers</name>
        <occupation>dancer</occupation>
        <partner rdf:resource="http://www.example.org/fred"/>
    </rdf:Description>
    <rdf:Description rdf:about="http://www.example.org/fred">
        <name>Fred Astaire</name>
        <occupation>dancer</occupation>
        <likes rdf:resource="http://www.example.org/ice-cream"/>
    </rdf:Description>
</rdf:RDF>
```

W3C Support

That they produce logical representations of triples doesn't mean triple stores necessarily have triple-like internal implementations. Most triple stores, however, are unified by their support for Semantic Web technology such as RDF and SPARQL. Though there's nothing particularly special about RDF as a means of serializing linked data, it is endorsed by the W3C and therefore benefits from being widely understood and well documented. The query language SPARQL benefits from similar W3C patronage.

In the graph database space there is a similar abundance of innovation around graph serialization formats [e.g., GEOFF (*http://geoff.nigelsmall.net/*)] and inferencing query languages [e.g., the Cypher query language (*http://docs.neo4j.org/chunked/milestone/cypher-query-lang.html*) that we use throughout this book]. The key difference is that at this point these innovations do not enjoy the patronage of a well-regarded body like the W3C, though they do benefit from strong engagement within their user and vendor communities.

Triple stores fall under the general category of graph databases because they deal in data that—once processed—tends to be logically linked. They are not, however, "native" graph databases, because they do not support index-free adjacency, nor are their storage engines optimized for storing property graphs. Triple stores store triples as independent artifacts, which allows them to scale horizontally for storage, but precludes them from rapidly traversing relationships. To perform graph queries, triple stores must create connected structures from independent facts, which adds latency to each query. For these reasons, the sweet spot for a triple store is analytics, where latency is a secondary consideration, rather than OLTP (responsive, online transaction processing systems).

Although graph databases are designed predominantly for traversal performance and executing graph algorithms, it is possible to use them as a backing store behind a RDF/SPARQL endpoint. For example, the Blueprints SAIL API (*https://github.com/tinkerpop/blueprints/wiki/ Sail-Implementation*) provides an RDF interface to several graph databases. In practice this implies a level of functional isomorphism between graph databases and triple stores. However, each store type is suited to a different kind of workload, with graph databases being optimized for graph workloads and rapid traversals.

Index

Symbols

@GET annotation, 80
@POST annotation, 80
@BeforeClass annotation, 86

A

A* algorithm, 173
access control, 104, 116–124
ACID transactions, 100
    BASE vs., 184–186
ad hoc structures, 103
aggregate store model (NOSQL databases), 15–17
    column families as, 194
    Domain-Driven Design, 195
    performance with connected data, 21
    query vs. processing, 195
agility, 8
allowed boolean property, 119
Amazon, 189
Amazon Web Services (AWS), 79
amortized view, 36
anchors, 28
anonymous nodes, 46
anti-patterns, 61
APIs, 74, 150–154
    Beans, 151
    Core, 151

    Kernel, 151
    server extensions, 78
    Traversal, 152
application
    architecture, 73–82
    performance testing, 90
    server clusters, 75
application programming interface (API), 9
arbitrary depth paths, 46
ASCII, 46
authorizations, 104
    controling, 116–124
availability
    of data, 157–159
    performance and, 94
average request time, 97

B

balanced closures, 180
balanced triadic closures, 179
BASE vs. ACID transactions, 184–186
Beans APIs, 151
best-first searches, 172
bidirectional relationships, 115
Big Table (Google), 192, 195
Blueprints SAIL API, 200
bound nodes, 45
breadth-first search, 163, 174
browser-based applications, 116

We'd like to hear your suggestions for improving our indexes. Send email to index@oreilly.com.

O

O-notation of performance measurements, 17
object cache, 149
online analytical processing (OLAP), 4
online transactional processing (OLTP), 4
optimization
    criteria, 93
    performance, 95–96
organization data, 180

P

partitioning, 80
Partner, Jonas, 20
path based query languages, 27
pathological graph topologies, 172
paths, 28
    finding with Dijkstra algorithm, 164–172
    in graphs, 20
pattern nodes, 46
Pegasus, 7
per-request transactions, 76
performance, 8, 94–96, 99
    applications, testing, 90
    joins and, 117
    O-notation as measurement of, 17
    optimization criteria, 94
    optimization options, 95–96
    queries and, 89
    testing, 89–93
platform independence, 75
POST request, 80
precise algorithms, 101
predictive analysis, 163
predictive modeling, 174–180
PREVIOUS relationships, 71
processing engines, 5
production deployment, 93
properties, 4, 26
property graph model, 26
    characteristics of, 196
    graph theory and, 174
    using, 8
property index file, 148
property store (Neo4j), 147
purchase history, modeling with graphs, 21
PUT request, 80

Q

queries
    beginning, 45
    localizing, 46
query chaining, 49
query languages, 27
query performance, 99
    testing, 89
querying, 27–31

R

R-tree (geospatial coordinate representations),
    22, 102
Rails, 36
RAM (random access memory), 95
rational layering, 178
RavenDB, 185
RDBMS (relational database management sys-
    tems), 25
RDF (triple stores), 199
read patterns, 149
read vs. write traffic, 80
recommendation algorithms, building, 101
recovering
    data, 156
    state of the graph, 72
redundancy, 97
    optimization criteria, 94
regression tests, 73
relating nodes, 44
relational database management systems
    (RDBMS), 25
relational databases
    graph databases, 18–23
    graph model vs., 37
    indexes vs. document stores, 187
    mimicking connected data in, 11–14
    performance with connected data, 21
relational modeling, 33–36
    graphs compared to, 31–40
relational sets vs. graphs, 30
relational stores, 33
relationship chain, 145
relationship store (Neo4j), 145
    doubly linked lists in, 146
relationships, 6
    add new, 73
    building structure with, 64

About the Authors

Ian Robinson works on research and development for future versions of the Neo4j graph database, having previously served as Neo Technology's Director of Customer Success, where he worked with customers to design and develop graph database solutions. He is a coauthor of *REST in Practice* (O'Reilly) and a contributor to *REST: From Research to Practice* (Springer) and *Service Design Patterns* (Addison-Wesley). He blogs at *http://iansrobinson.com* and tweets at @iansrobinson.

Dr. Jim Webber is Chief Scientist with Neo Technology, where he researches novel graph databases and writes open source software. Previously, Jim spent time working with big graphs like the Web for building distributed systems, which led him to being a coauthor on the book *REST in Practice* (O'Reilly). Jim is active in the development community, presenting regularly around the world. His blog is located at *http://jimwebber.org* and he tweets often at @jimwebber.

Emil Eifrem sketched the property graph model on a flight to Mumbai in 2000. As the CEO of Neo Technology and cofounder of the Neo4j project, he's devoted his professional life to building and evangelizing graph databases. Committed to sustainable open source, Emil guides Neo along a balanced path between free availability and commercial reliability. He plans to save the world with graphs and own Larry's yacht by the end of the decade. Emil tweets at @emileifrem.

Colophon

The animal on the cover of *Graph Databases* is a European octopus (*Eledone cirrhosa*), also known as a lesser octopus or horned octopus. The European octopus is native to the rocky coasts of Ireland and England, but can also be found in the Atlantic Ocean, North Sea, and Mediterranean Sea. It mainly resides in depths of 10 to 15 meters, but has been noted as far down as 800 meters. Its identifying features include its reddish-orange color, white underside, granulations on its skin, and ovoid mantle.

The European octopus eats primarily crabs and other crustaceans. Many fisheries in the Mediterranean and North Seas often unintentionally catch the European octopus. The species is not subject to stock assessment or quota control, so they can be consumed. However, their population has increased in these areas in recent years due in part to the overfishing of larger predatory fish.

The European octopus can grow to be between 12 and 40 centimeters, which it reaches in about one year. It has a relatively short life span of less than five years. Compared to the *octopus vulgaris* (or common octopus), the European octopus breeds at a much lower rate, laying on average 1,000 to 5,000 eggs.

The cover image is from Dover Pictorial Archive. The cover font is Adobe ITC Garamond. The text font is Adobe Minion Pro; the heading font is Adobe Myriad Condensed; and the code font is Dalton Maag's Ubuntu Mono.

Have it your way.

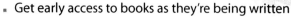

Get even more for your money.

Join the O'Reilly Community, and register the O'Reilly books you own. It's free, and you'll get:

- $4.99 ebook upgrade offer
- 40% upgrade offer on O'Reilly print books
- Membership discounts on books and events
- Free lifetime updates to ebooks and videos
- Multiple ebook formats, DRM FREE
- Participation in the O'Reilly community
- Newsletters
- Account management
- 100% Satisfaction Guarantee

Signing up is easy:

1. **Go to: oreilly.com/go/register**
2. **Create an O'Reilly login.**
3. **Provide your address.**
4. **Register your books.**

Note: English-language books only

To order books online:
oreilly.com/store

For questions about products or an order:
orders@oreilly.com

To sign up to get topic-specific email announcements and/or news about upcoming books, conferences, special offers, and new technologies:
elists@oreilly.com

For technical questions about book content:
booktech@oreilly.com

To submit new book proposals to our editors:
proposals@oreilly.com

O'Reilly books are available in multiple DRM-free ebook formats. For more information:
oreilly.com/ebooks

O'REILLY®

Spreading the knowledge of innovators   oreilly.com

CPSIA information can be obtained at www.ICGtesting.com
Printed in the USA
BVOW01s1408180314

348021BV00001B/1/P